NOTES FROM THE
DOCTOR

THE
60 DAY
DEVOTIONAL
TREATMENT PLAN
FOR THE
SPIRIT

Thank You!

D. Ca...

REV. DR. CHARLEY HAMES, JR.

SPIRITDRIVEN
PUBLISHING

Spirit Driven Publishing ™
JP Designs Art, cover design
Paraclete Press, interior design & layout
Sarah Kovac, editor

First Edition
Printed in the United States of America

The title is also available in eBook and Audio.

Library of Congress Control Number: 2020910157

ISBN: 978-1-7923-4134-2

Dedication Page

I dedicate *Notes from the Doctor* to Alice Freeman; Danny Clark; Richard Daniels, II; and Reverends Michael Johnson and Vicky Stoneham. I am grateful for these leaders who have invested in the kingdom of God with me as we ushered others into the presence of Christ!

I also dedicate this book to Bishops Henry M Williamson, Sr; James B Walker; and Bobby R Best; who allowed me to serve one of the best congregations the heavens have to offer the world: Beebe Memorial Cathedral CME.

These Bishops, along with many others, have played a significant role in my leadership development, which taught me the grace to figure out this thing called ministry!

To my three children Charles Jonathon, Elijah Immanuel, and Jael Deon. This is your legacy: to continue to give your best.

Finally, to my amazing wife, Michelle. Thank you for your confidence in me! Love you always.

Table of Contents

Before You Begin This Work

Here is a little background for the inspiration for this work. For over sixteen years, I have spent time sharing inspirational nuggets with the San Francisco Bay Area through radio on 102.9 KBLX FM. I have had many people write or call my office to request what they heard me share over radio waves for their personal devotional use. *Notes from the Doctor* was sparked by what I shared out of my love to inspire people to live better lives. I hope that this 60 Day Devotional Treatment Plan for the Spirit will encourage you, stretch you, and affirm you in a way that will uplift your essence and transform your heart. So, let's begin!

I am so grateful that you have chosen to spend the next 60 days in the Notes from the Doctor devotional. Here are a few points that I hope will encourage you as you begin your experience:

- **COMMIT TO A TIME**

Spending a few moments alone with God the first thing in the morning can be most suitable for setting the tone for your day. But, if you're not a morning person, choose the best time for your schedule. Whatever time you select, stick with it and make it a time that means the most to you.

- **DECIDE TO ENGAGE**

Plan to use this book for the next 60 days, setting aside deliberate and un-distracted time to form a habit of engaging with God daily. If you miss a day or two, pick up where you left off. This is not designed to be punitive, but an encouraging experience to build your relationship with God. So don't quit. Every moment you invest in this book will be worth it.

- **CHOOSE A SPECIAL PLACE**

Pick the most fitting place you can find away from disturbances. No phones. No devices. No television. Make sure you have a serene environment, and engage your focus on God.

- **READ AND READ AGAIN**

Take in all the content. Ask God for revelation as you read the scriptures, devotionals, and prayer. Take your time and enjoy the moment.

- **PRAY**

Allow time for God to speak to you, and for you to talk with God. Be truthful. Be specific. If you have never really prayed before or are uncomfortable, I have provided a prayer for each day. Learning to pray will revolutionize your life and your spiritual growth. The more you pray, the easier it will become!

- **WRITE**

Write your thoughts and reflections after working through each devotional. Your writing provides time in the Bible. It also gives a mental picture of crucial verses to memorize. Finally, it helps in remembering **THE TREATMENT PLAN**.

- **USE IN A SMALL GROUP**

This book would be good to share in a small group to discuss the intent of the material and share insights you gleaned from the book. This is your opportunity to make a connection, build authentic relationships, and make a difference in the lives of others.

Behind Closed Doors

THE SYMPTOM

What if they find out the truth about me?

THE DIAGNOSIS

You never know what someone is dealing with behind closed doors. We only identify what we see or perceive to be real.

THE PRESCRIPTION

On the evening of that first day of the week, when the disciples were together, with the doors locked for fear of the Jewish leaders, Jesus came and stood among them and said, "Peace be with you!"

After he said this, he showed them his hands and side. The disciples were overjoyed when they saw the Lord.

Again Jesus said, "Peace be with you! As the Father has sent me, I am sending you." And with that he breathed on them and said, "Receive the Holy Spirit. If you forgive anyone's sins, their sins are forgiven; if you do not forgive them, they are not forgiven."
John 20:19-23

THE TREATMENT PLAN

It is incredible to me that people can be confident, poised, and bold in public—and you would think they are this way all the time—but in reality, the individual you see and interact with is a personal representative. We never get to see the real them, because the authentic person is locked behind a closed door. In that personal space they have nowhere to hide from the issues they face relationally, spiritually, and physically. It is behind the closed door that fears become confident, anxiety is audacious, and our pride becomes presumptuous. They don't know where to turn because, as with the COVID-19 pandemic of early 2020, there is a sense of confusion and fear, as they aren't sure where it came from or how it would alter their life. I want to offer a remedy for the times when life becomes unbearable in your core self: the very place you ought to experience the most harmony. Jesus shows up with the antidote that you can use to come out of your spiritual quarantine. It is His peace! When you use His peace, it pries loose the grip of abuse in your life and puts your panic in its place. Also, beyond His peace, He gives you the Holy Spirit so you can walk in authority and the power to forgive those who've hurt you. Yes, when you forgive it releases them, but it also frees you!

THE FOLLOW-UP

Lord,

Open the doors to my heart, which have been closed by hurt and pain. Give me peace that exists beyond the portals of my past and allows me to enjoy peace of mind in any situation. Nothing can keep me from the freedom I've found in you! Amen.

Wearing the Mask

THE SYMPTOM

Do they love the real me, or the person they think I am?

THE DIAGNOSIS

Life is a real challenge when you are afraid to reveal who you are because you have become comfortable living the life others want to see.

THE PRESCRIPTION

"We refuse to wear masks and play games. We don't maneuver and manipulate behind the scenes. And we don't twist God's Word to suit ourselves. Rather, we keep everything we do and say out in the open, the whole truth on display, so that those who want to can see and judge for themselves in the presence of God." *2 Corinthians 4:2*

Peterson, E. H. (2005). *The Message: The Bible in Contemporary Language.* Colorado Springs, CO: NavPress.

THE TREATMENT PLAN

As children, we found ways to protect ourselves from being hurt, diminished, disappointed, and broken. We put on armor; we used our thoughts, emotions, and behaviors as weapons; and we learned how to make ourselves scarce or even invisible. Now, as adults, we realize that to live with courage, purpose, and connection—to be the person whom we long to be—we must again be exposed. However, it is not that easy! It is easier for us to be guarded and hard than to be vulnerable and revealed.

The word persona is the Greek term for "stage mask." The mask is how we protect ourselves from the discomfort of fragility. Masks make us feel safer even as they suffocate the wearer. Behind the cover, we can be confident, secure, and successful, although no one really knows who we are. We wear the mask because it is easier to live an illusion than to deal with the fact that we don't have it all together.

Yes, we are mask wearers in carefully framed selfies, well executed Instagram Stories, curated Snapchats, and trending tweets. However, when the camera is turned off, the phone is silent, and the battery has run out, you still have to deal with the demons that cause you to live in conflict and disguise.

The irony is that when we're standing across from someone hidden or shielded by masks, we feel frustrated and disconnected. Noted author and motivational speaker Brené Brown says, "The difficult thing is that vulnerability is the first thing I look for in you and the last thing I'm willing to show you. In you, it's courage and daring. In me, it's weakness."

Allow me to share a spiritual cure for when life leaves you in a place feeling exposed and unprotected: The higher your vulnerability is, the more license you have to live your truth. No more hiding in the shadows of doubt and disgust—you are free to live. The moment you experience this freedom, you will realize that those who you thought had it all together were just like you: struggling to breathe behind a pretty mask.

THE FOLLOW-UP

Dear Lord Jesus,

Remove the cover of doubt that keeps me wrapped in fantasy instead of reality. Expose my weakness that it may become my strength, and give me the courage to wear my suit of truth! In Your Name, I pray. Amen.

● ●

_____

_____

_____

_____

Hard Work

THE SYMPTOM

I believe I can achieve this goal. I only have to wait for it to happen.

THE DIAGNOSIS

People believe that positive thoughts alone will be enough to get them to their goals. But thoughts can become horror stories if they are not followed up with hard work.

THE PRESCRIPTION

You will eat the fruit of your labor;

blessings and prosperity will be yours.

Psalm 128:2

THE TREATMENT PLAN

You cannot dream yourself into a character; you must hammer and shape yourself into what you should become. It is terrific to have dreams, but dreams can become nightmares when you don't put in the work to make your dream a reality. Here is a newsflash: If you want something that will be worth it and last beyond a moment, you will have to work for it. I know this may be something that you may not want to hear, but it's actually great news. You can become a success story, and it first starts with you.

How badly you want something dictates how hard you'll work at it! If you do not go after what you want, you'll never have it. If you do not ask, the answer will always be no. If you do not step forward, you will stay in the same place. There is no elevator to success. You will have to take the stairs. Yes, it is called "work" for a reason, but eventually, it will pay off! God rewards those who work hard and blesses those who show faithfulness. I heard this adage that blessed me that I will share with you: "When you feel like quitting, think about why you started."

THE FOLLOW-UP

Dear God,

Enterprise my vision for my life, help me to act on what I see, and assist me in performing my best until my goals become my reality. Bless me to strive and work until my assignment is complete! Amen.

My Point of View

THE SYMPTOM

I see it as I see it!

THE DIAGNOSIS

Everyone will see something different, determined by their focus, attitude, and current mood or situation. Things can go sideways if you buy into the reflection that isn't your reality!

THE PRESCRIPTION

For now we see in a mirror dimly, but then face to face. Now I know in part; then I shall know fully, even as I have been fully known.

1 Corinthians 13: 12

The Holy Bible: English Standard Version. (2016). Wheaton, IL: Crossway Bibles.

THE TREATMENT PLAN

In 1878, Margaret Wolfe Hungerford wrote this phrase that has lasted until this day: "Beauty is in the eye of the beholder." She expressed so succinctly that the perception of beauty is subjective—what one person finds beautiful another may not. This truth was also demonstrated in Walt Disney's classic Snow White and Seven Dwarfs, when the evil queen engages in her famous dialogue with the magic mirror.

In my hermeneutic suspicion, I must dismiss the subliminal message that plagues a beautiful story that whiteness is considered the "fairest." We know that one's skin tone doesn't determine how beautiful you are; what defines your beauty is how you love and how lovable you are. We recognize that some of the most beautiful people on the planet have been kissed by nature's sun!

"Mirror, mirror, on the wall, who's the fairest of them all?"

What does a mirror do? It mirrors or reflects objects or a scene back. It merely throws up a reflection of whatever happens to be situated just in front of it. It is a snapshot of a specific area. It does not contain information about the time or place or context of anything that is going on outside of this perimeter. The mirror is impartial to what it reflects back. The mirror is entirely objective. It only reflects what we project. Yet, how we view what the mirror shows us tells the story of what we see. It is only when we assign meaning to the reflection that we begin to find out "who is the fairest of us all." And then again, who is the judge of what is fair or not? Well, if you happen to be looking into the mirror, the fair one will be YOU.

The mirror, my brothers and sisters, is a useful symbol to astutely suggest that the reflection we fall in love with sets our expectations of reality. We like to see our lives from the best possible angle instead of taking in the 360-degrees of reality we are experiencing! In order to accept the truth of the reflection, we will have to break up with our point of view. Until that breakup happens, it will be challenging for us to have a productive relationship with ourselves and others.

THE FOLLOW-UP

Dear Father,

Help us to attract what we expect, reflect what we desire, become what we respect, and to mirror what we admire.

In Jesus' Name, Amen.

Not Close Enough

THE SYMPTOM

"Learn the difference between connection and attachment. Connection gives you power; attachment sucks the life out of you."
—Anonymous

THE DIAGNOSIS

More often than not, we are only partially attached to the source of power that provides for our comfort, joy, and peace. As a result, the connection we have isn't stable enough to sustain the life we desire to live!

THE PRESCRIPTION

"These people honor me with their lips,
but their hearts are far from me."
Matthew 15:8

THE TREATMENT PLAN

A few years ago, I received an urgent message from my cable provider telling me that I had a severe issue with my cable system and that it would eventually affect my whole neighborhood.

They seemed anxious to fix the problem, and the very next day they showed up. I asked the service technician, "Can you tell me the problem that I am experiencing?" He politely said, "Dr. Hames, you have an ingress in your system which has the potential of ruining your connection along with your neighbors." The service technician started to test my system by connecting his monitor to my cable line, and within a few minutes he found the issue.

The issue was that one of my cable lines was attached to the cable box, but it wasn't fully connected. I said to myself, how is that possible? The technician explained that because the coax cable cord was in proximity of the outlet, it was close enough to get an intermittent signal. As a consequence of being close but never fully engaged, it had the potential to ruin the whole system. **It was close enough to receive the signal, but not connected enough to sustain the power!** Ingress.

In our scripture above, some people spoke of God yet failed to honor him. They esteemed the views of corrupt humanity too highly. The result was that they nullified and made void the Word of God.

What about you? Have you been surfing the web to catch clips of sermons, but not really taking the time to listen for what God has to say concerning your life? Your searching keeps your interest, but your relationship with God gives you power! My spiritual treatment for you is to not settle for a casual connection with God when He is offering you a lifelong relationship. To say you know Him is useful, but it's most important that he knows you. Stay connected!

THE FOLLOW-UP

Dear Lord,

Mitigate our faulty connection, alleviate our need to remain on the surface of our relationship with you, and ease our minds to know you love us beyond the moment; but for eternity. Amen.

You Decide

THE SYMPTOM

I can never make up my mind, and it makes me miserable.

THE DIAGNOSIS

Indecisiveness is negligence in a costume. Many people never reach their destination because they fail to make a decision.

THE PRESCRIPTION

If any of you lacks wisdom, you should ask God, who gives generously to all without finding fault, and it will be given to you.
James 1:5

THE TREATMENT PLAN

One decision can alter your existence and ultimately change your life. You are only one "yes" or "no" away from a different experience. We make thousands of choices every day on autopilot, quickly and without a mistake. Yet we don't give a second thought to the incredible human ability to make decisions on the fly until we falter, and something goes wrong.

Whether you believe you can fulfill your assignment or not, you are right! No one can determine the consequences of your actions better than you. In other words, what we think about something often creates the outcome we experience. I know you feel you can't change. Or you don't want to change. Or the world won't change. When you think this way, you will remain powerless to improve the course of your life.

Life can become what we make it with God's help. My spiritual plan for you is to consider asking God about your next move. You must choose to take the chance if you want anything in your life to change! You will have to accept the fact that you have authority and can determine the outcome of your situation: When it comes to your goals, is your approach "One day…" or "Day one"? You decide.

THE FOLLOW-UP

Dear God,

I am asking You to give me the wisdom to know when to step forward or to move back. Provide the answer I need—whether or not I want to hear or receive it. In Your Son's name, Amen.

● ●

_____

_____

_____

_____

_____

_____

_____

_____

_____

_____

_____

_____

_____

A Prayer that Works

THE SYMPTOM

I am not sure if things can turn around because I am constantly defeated. My hope is depleted.

THE DIAGNOSIS

You feel like your prayers aren't sufficient for the battles you are experiencing. You are going through the motions because you know you should, but you are at a loss because nothing you do seems to be helping matters.

THE PRESCRIPTION

"No weapon forged against you will prevail,
and you will refute every tongue that accuses you.
This is the heritage of the servants of the Lord,
and this is their vindication from me,"
declares the Lord.
Isaiah 54:17

THE TREATMENT PLAN

I have been in situation after situation wondering when things were going to get better. I know you have heard before that "prayer changes things," and it does, but you need to understand what kind of prayer changes things. In my experience and spiritual walk, the type of prayer that makes a difference in your life is when you pray for the enemy to be defeated and destroyed concerning you! Too often today, believers gather for prayer as though attending a concert or a party. There is a little sense of urgency and crisis because most of us are content in our Christian walk.

However, you may get to the place in your walk that you get tired of being tied up by the enemy's tactics. Once you get tired of the enemy destroying the very thing that you have worked so hard to achieve, then you are ready, my friend, to change your prayers.

Change looks like this: Say to yourself, *I am no longer going to pray for things, positions, and privilege; but from now on, I am going to pray that the enemy will be crushed in my life. Yes, no weapon formed against me shall prosper!*

THE FOLLOW-UP

Dear Jehovah Nissi,

Send your angels to survey my situation, protect the gateways to my faith, and seize the opportunity to have victory in the areas of my life where I have experienced defeat. In Jesus' Name, Amen.

Worry Never Works

THE SYMPTOM

Worry is creating a world of anxiety in my mind, and I'm tired of living there.

THE DIAGNOSIS

"Worrying is like sitting in a rocking chair: It gives you something to do, but it doesn't get you anywhere."
—*English proverb*

THE PRESCRIPTION

Do not be anxious about anything, but in every situation, by prayer and petition, with thanksgiving, present your requests to God. And the peace of God, which transcends all understanding, will guard your hearts and your minds in Christ Jesus.
Philippians 4:6-7

THE TREATMENT PLAN

Most of the time, what you are worrying about will never come to pass. If you have lived long enough, you have experienced and know this to be true. Even though you have access to archives of testimonies that suggest that you shouldn't worry, it doesn't take away your capacity to over-analyze situations and circumstances. Worry preoccupies your mind with thoughts that deaden the psyche and it tries to control your outcomes.

As a consequence, what you are working on becomes sidetracked by negative views of endless possibilities, none of which you can control. My advice when this starts to happen is to present your request to God, because He can do far more than you would ever dream. Followers of the faith who carry their burdens to the Lord will find peace and rest in their spirits. This peace will stand at the door and guard your heart and mind, so that anxious care and worry cannot enter. It is a beautiful peace from the Lord that unbelievers cannot find and cannot explain. So, whatever it is, give it over to the Lord, and I know He can work it out for you! This, too, shall pass!

THE FOLLOW-UP

Dear Lord Jesus,

   Eliminate the wall of worry. Drop the adverse thoughts that saturate my mind and free me to live grateful that you are in control! In Your Name, Amen.

The Advantage

THE SYMPTOM

If I get rid of my bad habits and vices, who will I be?

THE DIAGNOSIS

The evil that goes unchecked can do serious damage.

THE PRESCRIPTION

You intended to harm me, but God intended it for good…
Genesis 50:20a

THE TREATMENT PLAN

On May 6, 2013, there was a story that made national news that rocked our country. The city of Cleveland witnessed a miracle when Amanda Berry called 911 from a neighbor's phone. "I've been kidnapped and been missing for ten years. I'm here. I'm free now," Berry, now 33, told the 911 operator. Two fellow captives were found alive in a two-story home in a Cleveland neighborhood. Vanished for nearly a decade, their story is a miracle within itself.

These abused women feared for their lives with no hope that their situation would change. They were tormented, lived in horrifying conditions, and were punished if they tried to leave. But then one day their captor left home to visit a nearby McDonald's restaurant. Amanda Berry noticed that he had forgotten to lock the "big inside door" on his way out. For several years, he never forgot to lock the door, but this day was the one time he did. She took advantage of his mistake.

Hear this truth: her enemy's mistake became her opportunity for deliverance. The moment her enemy slipped up, that's when Berry got up and found the boldness to call out for help. Listen, my friend, the enemy will eventually slip up in your life and make a mistake of underestimating your strength and value. When this happens, that's when it is your time and opportunity to take control and be free from that which had you bound. Remember, what they meant for evil God will use for your good! Seize the opportunity!

THE FOLLOW-UP

Dear Lord,

> *Break away the evil that keeps me locked in, and allow me to slip away from this place of captivity. Free me to be the person that you made in your image. In Jesus' Name, Amen.*

Patience is Key

THE SYMPTOM

In my impatience, I struggle to make thoughtful, wise decisions.

THE DIAGNOSIS

The more you try to force your way into your success, the more significant problems will arise as a result. Developing patience will permit you to allow some things to unfold the way they are meant to.

THE PRESCRIPTION

Stand firm, and you will win life.
Luke 21:19

THE TREATMENT PLAN

Have you discovered that people want everything to happen in an instant? If we walk into a building and the Wi-Fi isn't super fast, we get irritated. If our text message or Snapchat takes longer than two seconds to send, we become frustrated and impatient.

The point is that our culture expects results right away and access to what we desire immediately. Moreover, our surrounding gadgets, systems, and services are only moving quicker to meet our expectations. When we get instant results and convenience in some parts of our life, we expect other areas of our life to work just as quickly and easily.

This expectation is not reality! Your life doesn't work like this all of the time. How many relationships that we rushed into became "situationships" because we weren't patient? You find yourself tolerating individuals with whom you have nothing in common, and often they stay in your life longer than needed. The Greek proverb said it best: "One minute of patience is worth ten years of peace." I want to encourage you that the one who masters patience masters everything!

THE FOLLOW-UP

Gracious God,

Slow down the pace of my aspirations, set my goals to your divine speed, and lead me to a destiny that you have ordained for my life. You said in your word, "A thousand years in your sight are like a day that has just gone by, or like a watch in the night." (Psalm 90:1) Give me the patience so that I can win. In Jesus' Name, Amen.

Think Big

THE SYMPTOM

I am always disappointed in myself. I don't think I can accomplish anything big with my life.

THE DIAGNOSIS

You are limited by expectations that you place on yourself. God has placed a dream inside you, but you look for others to affirm it.

THE PRESCRIPTION

Jesus looked at them and said, "With man, this is impossible, but with God all things are possible."
Matthew 19:26

THE TREATMENT PLAN

We will always tend to fulfill our own expectations of ourselves. If you feel you can't do more, you won't, and if you think you can do more, you will. You must understand that you become your own best example of what is possible. Your constraints and achievements are based, for the most part, on the assumptions you entertain about yourself. Your focus tends to become your reality!

I've seen it over and over: so many of us are convinced we are incapable of achieving great things, so we aim for the mediocre. If you're not willing to fail, you're guaranteed stay average, at best.

If you want to grow into an extraordinary version of yourself, you must be willing to fail. Don't let small thinking cut your life down to size. Think big. Aim high. Act bold and see just how big you can blow up your life. David J. Schwarts says, "Belief big." The size of your belief determines the size of your success. Think of little goals and expect little achievements. Your life only gets better when you get better. So, my challenge to you is to think big! Think so big that what you are thinking scares you into the knowledge that only God could deliver those results.

Think big and don't listen to people who tell you it can't be done. We accept the reality that we believe we deserve. Life's too short to think minor thoughts about a major vision for your life. If people aren't calling you crazy, you aren't thinking big enough. Your only limit is you! Your future is bright, and your destiny will be incredible when you shift your thinking to the huge possibilities that God has for you! I believe it can happen. What about you?

THE FOLLOW-UP

Dear Creator of Divine Possibilities,

Remove the box of limitations placed upon me, discard cynical thoughts, exclude small-minded people from my vision, and push the envelope to my purpose. In Jesus' Name, Amen.

Loving You Should Be Easy!

THE SYMPTOM

I am looking for love in all the wrong places, I never took the time to seek God and to start with myself.

THE DIAGNOSIS

Many people do not create the necessary habit of exploring their relationship with God, which leads to loving themselves. Instead, that they look for someone else to fulfill what God can only do, thus creating insatiable appetite that never goes away.

THE PRESCRIPTION

We love because he first loved us.

1 John 4:19

THE TREATMENT PLAN

This is an important lesson I've learned about relationships: Until you come to the truth that you have to break up with the concept of you, it will be difficult for you to have a productive relationship with someone else.

Allow me to explain. I am fascinated with Greek mythology. The myth of the goddess is told in Book III of the *Metamorphoses*.[1] This myth tells the story of a "talkative nymph" named Echo, whom the goddess Venus admires for her brilliant voice.

When Echo tricks and angers Juno (queen of the gods), Juno curses Echo by making her able only to finish a sentence someone else started. She is unable to say anything on her own. "Yet a chatterbox, had no other use of speech than she has now, that she could repeat only the last words out of many." Thus, her name is Echo.

She falls in love with Narcissus, but she cannot speak to him. Eventually, Echo's presence is revealed to Narcissus, who, after a comic yet tragic scene,

---

1   https://ovid.lib.virginia.edu/trans/Metamorph3.htm#476975712

rejects her love. Echo prays, in her mind, of this to Venus, who makes Echo disappear, until she "remains a voice," and "is heard by all."

Then, Narcissus goes on to fall in love with himself and wastes away with love for himself, as Echo did earlier. Echo symbolizes the inherent danger of wanting what you can't or shouldn't have. Echo's problem is that she can't let go of her fascination for Narcissus, even after Narcissus has rejected her. Have you ever wanted something you couldn't have? When you become fascinated with no restraints, it almost costs you more than what it was worth! Can I give you a bit of advice? You don't need to waste your time on someone who only wants you around when it fits their needs.

Yes, it is dangerous to fall in love with Narcissus even if you are Narcissus! It is dangerous to be intoxicated by the reflection of your desires to the extent that you miss the opportunity for genuine and real connection. You ask God to send you your soul mate, and God said I did, but you keep calling him "best friend."

You will lose yourself trying to hold on to someone who doesn't care about losing you! Learn to love you; then, you can love someone else.

THE FOLLOW-UP

Dear Lord,

Develop within my heart the passion for loving myself. Expand my capacity to become satisfied with who I am, my flaws, my imperfections, and the stuff that no one else sees. Bless me, dear Jesus, so that I may evolve my potential to be ready to love someone beyond me. In Your Name, I pray, Amen.

Be Selective

THE SYMPTOM

I argue and fight so often that sometimes I can't even remember what I'm fighting for.

THE DIAGNOSIS

So many people like to argue, fuss, and fight for the sake of confrontation. Instead of cutting their losses, they are determined to stay in the fight just because they can.

THE PRESCRIPTION

Starting a quarrel is like breaching a dam;
so drop the matter before a dispute breaks out.
Proverbs 17:14

THE TREATMENT PLAN

Be selective with your battles, and you will quickly learn that peace of mind is better than being right. Often, people will engage in a dispute because they have been offended, hurt, or misunderstood. These could very well be one of these reasons they start the battle, but many times, people stay engaged long after this issue has been resolved.

Ask yourself this question: Do I have to be right all of the time? Proving yourself right means showing that the other person is wrong, and truth be told no one likes to be incorrect. Remember doing things for principle's sake could cause a lot of unnecessary problems in your relationships. If you spend all of your time fighting every battle that comes your way, you have determined that peace is not your mission. I don't know about you, but I value peace of mind over being right for the sake of being right any day of the week! For at the end, who cares? If it can't change your position, pay scale, or lifestyle, is it worth the fight?

THE FOLLOW-UP

Dear Lord Jesus,

Guide us to know when to pull out the gloves of our passion and oversee us when we must lay down the gauntlet of justice. Teach to know when to hold them, to know when to fold them, to know when to walk away, and know when to run! In Your Name, Amen.

Self-Respect

THE SYMPTOM

People don't think highly of me, and I tend to agree with them.

THE DIAGNOSIS

"It's not what you are that is holding you back. It's what you think you are not."

—*Anonymous*

When you have been disrespected for so long, the rejection you feel becomes normative. As a consequence, when something good happens to you, you feel as if you don't deserve it.

THE PRESCRIPTION

"Do not give dogs what is sacred; do not throw your pearls to pigs. If you do, they may trample them under their feet, and turn and tear you to pieces."

Matthew 7:6

THE TREATMENT PLAN

"What you allow is what will continue." This anonymous quote has both blessed and convicted me. It is a fact that you cannot control another person's behavior. Nonetheless, you do not have to condone, sanction, or authorize their mistreatment and disrespect of you. Remember, what you allow is what will continue. Stop giving power to people who don't know how to handle you with care! Love is not a reason to endure discourtesy. Do you know who are in the faith? God has made you as precious as a pearl! The pressures of life have formed you, and the roughness of your circumstances has shaped you. As a consequence, your brilliance is incomparable, and your beauty is undeniable.

Is there anything in your life that you would like to stop and no longer allow?

I discovered that people treat you the way you empower them to do so. My word of advice to you is that if you don't value yourself, others will continue to devalue who you are. If you allow the wrong and the hurt to keep playing out in your life, you will continue to move farther away from the joy and happiness that you could be experiencing right now. Your life is meant to have positivity and delight. Don't make time for anything less!

THE FOLLOW-UP

Dear Eternal God,

Block those who don't value my purpose, check those who refuse to see the value in me, and terminate the relationships that no longer serve the best interest of my humanity. In Your Name, Amen.

Emotional Restraint

THE SYMPTOM

I struggle to control my emotions and sometimes my anger is over the top.

THE DIAGNOSIS

"Flying off the handle sometimes causes hammers and humans to lose their heads, as well as their effectiveness."
—*Williams Arthur Ward*

THE PRESCRIPTION

My dear brothers and sisters, take note of this: Everyone should be quick to listen, slow to speak and slow to become angry
James 1:19

THE TREATMENT PLAN

Warren Edward Buffett, who is a business magnate, investor, and philanthropist, said, "You will continue to suffer if you have an emotional reaction to everything that is said to you. True power is sitting back and observing things with logic. True power is restraint. If words control you, that means everyone else can control you. Breathe and allow things to pass."

I learned to practice restraint in my leadership style and also in my ministry, and it has blessed my life tremendously. People will challenge you and provoke you to see how you will react. It is critical to understand that just because people come at you in the wrong manner doesn't mean that you must react emotionally. It doesn't matter whether someone cut you off while you were driving in your car or whether a stranger insulted you in front of your family. Your greatest gift to yourself is the gift of emotional restraint.

Your power lies in your ability to control your emotional reaction. The moment you master control of your emotions is the instant that other people lose their command over you! Real power is taking a step back using your mind and not your passion to determine your response. If words can control you, that means everyone else can. Take back your authority and demonstrate restraint. Someone will become delivered by how they see you respond to a tough situation.

THE FOLLOW-UP

Dear Lord God,

Simmer my emotions, stew my grievances, and braise my anger so that my testimony will not be disrupted by a moment of conflict.

In Jesus' Name, Amen.

● ●

Letting Go

THE SYMPTOM

I am holding on to hurt for too long because I feel like I have no other options. The longer I hold on the more I am drained and dangerous I become.

THE DIAGNOSIS

Holding on to hurt doesn't fix anything. In some cases, when it comes to the past, it actually makes things a lot worse.

THE PRESCRIPTION

Cast all your anxiety on him because he cares for you.
1 Peter 5:7

THE TREATMENT PLAN

One of the most joyful moments in life is when you find the strength to let go of what you can't change. When you release what you have been holding on to, it creates space for something more beneficial. You become free to be who God called you to be. The ability to let go is a key to unlock so many supernatural blessings in your life.

The longer you attempt to hold on to stuff, people, and predicaments, the more you'll be robbed of your ability to live well. I encourage you to say to yourself, "If I keep holding on to that person, place, or situation; it will eventually destroy me." Have you noticed how weighed down you feel now? How exhausted you feel? Consider the levels of stress that you have been enduring!

Allow me to offer you good news: God didn't call or appoint you to fix, change, or rescue anybody. Don't destroy yourself trying to fix someone else. Learn to do you and allow God to Him! God can do more with their development than you can do with their dilemma. Why are you still holding on? It's time for you to let go. The second that you do, the peace that you have missing will find its way back to you!

THE FOLLOW-UP

Dear Jehovah God,

Allow me to tap into your power. Penetrate the pain, so that I may be confident to let go of everything that is not useful for me. In Jesus' Name, Amen.

Privacy Matters

THE SYMPTOM

I share a lot about my life on social media, and sometimes it makes me feel less alone, but other times people's comments make me feel awful.

THE DIAGNOSIS

Oversharing leads to being criticized by those who don't deserve to have a voice in your matters.

THE PRESCRIPTION

And to make it your ambition to lead a quiet life: You should mind your own business and work with your hands, just as we told you...
1 Thessalonians 4:11

THE TREATMENT PLAN

A private life is a happy life. In the world of social media, where individuals are pressured every day into keeping up with the next person's highlight reel, everything about you doesn't have to be public. Nothing desirable will ever come out of everyone knowing your business. Not one thing!

You have to become comfortable with the reality that the less people know about you and your business, the more effective you will become. You will be free when you realize you don't need their affirmation. Stop treating everyone like you owe them something.

Shakespeare said, "Coins always make a sound, currency notes are always silent, so whenever your value increases keep yourself calm and silent." Some things you want to have as a treasure for those who love you and care about you, not those who secretly desire to be you! In the words of Denzel Washington, "just because you don't share it on social media doesn't mean you're not up to big things. Live it and stay low key." Just because it's not posted on social media doesn't mean it's not occurring for you. Privacy is priceless!

THE FOLLOW-UP

Dear Father,

Silence my loneliness, calm my need for affirmation, and hush those who feel that they need to be involved in my business and affairs.

Thank you for the gift of privacy! In Your Son's Name, I pray, Amen.

Rent Free

THE SYMPTOM

So many people have opinions on how I should live my life… I'm not sure who to listen to.

THE DIAGNOSIS

If you don't control your thinking, someone else is waiting to take control of you!

THE PRESCRIPTION

Do not conform to the pattern of this world, but be transformed by the renewing of your mind. Then you will be able to test and approve what God's will is—his good, pleasing, and perfect will.
Romans 12:2

THE TREATMENT PLAN

I don't know about you, but I am completely and totally amazed at how many people are invested in what you think and how you live. Most of the time the most curious are people who have not spent the time or energy investing in your life and purpose. Will Smith said, "Stop letting people who do so little for you control so much of your mind, feelings, and emotions." This is critical to your progress and growth as a person. Be cautious of who you allow to rent space in your head for free! If they are not adding to your life and depositing wisdom and knowledge, then time is overdue to give them and an eviction notice.

You need to raise the rent and kick them out of your life. That space in your faith and your head is prime real estate, and it should be given to those that can pour into your life. Don't be influenced by someone who doesn't value you, someone who envies you, or someone who will lie to you. Don't give mental space to anyone who would want to change you.

Allowing the wrong people in your head can mess up your miracle, hijack your healing, and distract your deliverance! Surround yourself with people who reflect who you want to be, how you want to feel, and where you want to go in life. These people are the ones who love you for you and care about your concerns and not solely their own. Allow these types of people to stay. Everyone else is window shopping!

THE FOLLOW-UP

Dear El-Shaddai,

Be a fence of protection around my mind, and guide my affairs that my life will be blessed with people who love me! In Jesus' Name, Amen.

Promised Victory

THE SYMPTOM

I am so tired. I am defeated. I cannot fight another battle.

THE DIAGNOSIS

Giving up before you start is a guaranteed defeat!

THE PRESCRIPTION

He said: "Listen, King Jehoshaphat and all who live in Judah and Jerusalem! This is what the Lord says to you: 'Do not be afraid or discouraged because of this vast army. For the battle is not yours, but God's.

2 Chronicles 20:15

THE TREATMENT PLAN

I know you have often wondered, "Why do I have conflict in my life when God has promised me victory?" You must understand that just because your relationship with God is secure and you are being blessed doesn't exempt you from friction. Promised victory doesn't eliminate your need to fight the battle! The battle that you are fighting gives you the necessary instruments to ensure what God promises. The contest is designed to strengthen your capacity to *retain* your promise. It has been my experience that when I am about to be blessed beyond the normal, that is when all hell breaks loose in my life.

As a consequence, the attacks from the enemy will intensify when God is getting ready to bless you in an extraordinary way. The battle you must fight is designed to sustain you for whatever comes next. There is a skillset that you develop in war. When you have gone through the struggle, there is a discernment you gain; acuteness develops, and astuteness is reinforced. You become wiser, more reliable, and more significant in the anointing.

If God just gave victory to you without a fight, you wouldn't appreciate it, you would feel entitled to it, and you would give up at the first sign of trouble. Please understand that the battle is not about the outcome—

it's about the process that develops you into the warrior that walks in the victory. So, go ahead and fight because you already know what the end will be when God is involved.

THE FOLLOW-UP

Dear Elohim,

Combat my resignation, contend my cause, and dispute my doubt so that I can see the value in the fight and also the promise! In Jesus' Name, Amen.

CEO of My Life

THE SYMPTOM

I am anxious and fearful about my life and what the future holds for me.

THE DIAGNOSIS

Virtually every waking moment of our lives, we are inundated by things we can't control. When we don't ever feel like we are in control, uncertainty and despair step in to manage our lives.

THE PRESCRIPTION

"For I know the plans I have for you," declares the Lord, "plans to prosper you and not to harm you, plans to give you hope and a future."
Jeremiah 29:11

THE TREATMENT PLAN

You may feel that you can't make a significant difference when it comes to your life. You take one step forward and three steps back—your dreams are turning into a nightmare because it feels like you can't get it together. As a result, you have grown to believe that things will not change. I respectfully disagree with you!

You have much more power over your life than you realize. It is not your status, position, or money that make you significant. You are the Chief Executive Officer (CEO) of your life. You are 100% responsible for your happiness, health, and wealth. A CEO has the ability and the authority to make the executive decisions for an organization or business. Your life is your company.

As the CEO, you must evaluate the people in your life and then exercise your authority to promote, demote, or terminate as necessary. Be disciplined about your goals and how you spend your time. Attract the essential individuals that can help you reach your objectives. Be disciplined about your self-care! Make sure you invest time to ensure that you are fit—physically, mentally, and emotionally—to lead the life you have always desired. If you do this, you are on your way to take your company (that's you!) to the next level. You will soar to new heights when you change your perception about your possibilities and take action! This is your season of personal worth and excellence!

THE FOLLOW-UP

Dear Adonai,

Govern my thoughts, demand my days, rule my relationships, and manage my perception so that I will realize all you have for me. In Jesus' Name, Amen.

The Diamond's Value

DAY 21

THE SYMPTOM

Is it possible for me to cope with it all? My problems are piling up and I don't feel like I can handle it much longer.

THE DIAGNOSIS

Many people don't know how to handle to day-to-day demands, and they fold under the pressure.

THE PRESCRIPTION

"On the day when I act," says the Lord Almighty, "they will be my treasured possession."

Malachi 3:17

THE TREATMENT PLAN

I remember listening to the fascinating story of a friend's encounter visiting South Africa. It was his first time in the motherland, and he wanted to show his wife the beauty and grandeur of the country. One of his first trips was to the place where they had some of the most precious stones in the whole world. As he arrived at the area to see the exquisite stones, he got out of his car.

He went into the jewelry storefront to see, as his wife waited with anticipation. He said, "I am here to see the owner." The gentleman replied and said, "I am he." My friend's face lit up and he said to the owner, "I am from the United States, please show us the best diamond you have." As my friend investigated the display cases, the owner said, "What you want to see is not these cases; please follow me."

They left the store and went into another building where they crowded into the small room. The owner said, "I keep it back here, and I want you to see it for yourself." He pulled out a rock from a crushed velvet garment. My friend marveled at the beauty of this diamond. He asked how much the diamond cost and whether he could buy it.

The owner immediately declined to sell and share the price, which was certainly in the high seven figures. My friend said, "I don't understand what makes this diamond so unique; it looks like others I have seen." The owner challenged him and demanded that he look through the loupe. My friend looked and saw that the diamond had a unique cut. The diamond's cut creates its value.

How do you see the cut that happened in your life? Do you view it as something that shouldn't have happened to you, or does it show you your value? The way you see your pain will determine how successful you shall become! In today's world, we are dealing with more stress and pressures daily. An unstable economy, health crisis, and rampant need for leadership have reshaped our universe and given us a new normal. We are all experiencing pressure on many levels. A diamond is simply a lump of coal that handles the pressure well. Let me ask, are you still shining?

How do you handle the pressure? Do you give in when things get too hard for you, or do you succeed despite the struggle? The way you treat the pressure will determine how you shine as a result of the stresses of life. Yes, you are designed to be a diamond, and the more substantial your cut is, the greater your value. Maybe God is allowing the demands of life to break away the unnecessary stuff so that the authentic you can shine through. Everybody wants to be a diamond, but very few are willing to get cut. Until life cuts you, you will never know your real value.

THE FOLLOW-UP

Dear God Eternal,

Cut through the pressures of my life, divide the losses, and form me into your image! Allow me to shine bright despite the pressures that come against me. In Jesus' Name, Amen.

Never Satisfied

THE SYMPTOM

I feel like my life isn't going anywhere. I don't expect much good from my future.

THE DIAGNOSIS

When you have no aspirations for your life, you have settled for mediocrity.

THE PRESCRIPTION

Blessed is the one
who does not walk in step with the wicked
or stand in the way that sinners take
or sit in the company of mockers,
but whose delight is in the law of the Lord,
and who meditates on his law day and night.
That person is like a tree planted by streams of water,
which yields its fruit in season
and whose leaf does not wither—
whatever they do prospers.
Psalm 1:1-3

THE TREATMENT PLAN

Never be satisfied with where you are, because that will be the day you stop trying hard to achieve. Yes, many people spend their whole lives trying to "arrive," and when they finally get "there," they become comfortable and forget the reason that they drove to this place. I had an aspiration to obtain my doctoral degree by the age of 30; I worked hard at this goal. I finished my master's degree within two and a half years, which should have taken three years. I was always working hard, not taking off summers so I could complete my degrees while maintaining a professional and family life.

I remember stepping onto the campus of Southern Methodist University with my cap and gown. My mother was sick at the time but managed to be present at one of the most important days of my life. In the back of my mind, I was asking the question, *What's next?* I worked all of these years for this moment, and within a few hours, it will be over. The Lord revealed to me that it wasn't about what I had obtained, but about the journey preparing me to have future stability and accomplishment. When you have become complacent, you're not growing! It is not so much about the destination as it is the journey!

God has placed within you everything you need to be successful and prosperous. The one thing that is necessary for you is to keep your drive and hunger that maintain your motivation to be your best! This one thing is your purpose. Your purpose is the fire you need to keep learning after the degrees are obtained and the positions have been held. I encourage you to hone your God-given purpose as it will remind you why you do what you do. If you don't challenge yourself enough, you'll inevitably feel unfulfilled. The ultimate place of happiness is living a life fulfilled and at peace. This is understanding your purpose!

THE FOLLOW-UP

Dear Jehovah Shammah,

Fill me with your purpose, charge me with Your Spirit, and saturate me with Your power! Remind me of my use in You that I may grow daily. In Your Name, I pray, Amen.

Grabbers Versus Givers

THE SYMPTOM

I feel like the people around me just take and take.

THE DIAGNOSIS

To some people, you only exist when they need something from you.

THE PRESCRIPTION

After this, his brother came out, with his hand grasping Esau's heel; so he was named Jacob. Isaac was sixty years old when Rebekah gave birth to them. *Genesis 25:26*

THE TREATMENT PLAN

The name Jacob comes from the biblical story of Jacob's birth, where he came out holding the heel of his twin brother, Esau. Jacob's name means "to follow, to be behind," but also "to supplant, circumvent, assail, overreach." This meaning played out in his behavior from birth until he had an encounter with God that changed his name. However, not everyone is as fortunate as Jacob; some do not seize the opportunity to transform nature and behavior.

An anonymous writer warns us to "know the difference between those who stay to feed the soil and those who come to grab the fruit."

In life, you will come across people who are grabbers and people who are givers. Allow me to deal with the grabbers first, as they are very similar to the nature of Jacob. Grabbers grab, grab, grab. This is all they know how to do! These people are only concerned with how much they can get from you without having to give too much of themselves. At all costs, please minimize your interactions with grabbers. The good news is that there are still givers in this world—people who see real value in contributing to others beyond themselves. There are still some people who see worth in giving and investing in others for goodness' sake.

Which raises the question: Which type of person are you? Are you a giver or a grabber? I prefer to hang out with the givers of life! Givers come into your life to feed your roots and your soul. Yes, they are going to take some fruit every now and again, but they're also going to share their fruit as well. As you travel through life, be prepared to encounter both grabbers and givers. Choose carefully who you associate with.

THE FOLLOW-UP

Dear Jehovah Jireh,

Provide balance for us to bless those who desire to give and discretion to see those who come to grab. Stockpile discernment so that when they both present themselves, it will be a blessing and not a lesson!

Deception

DAY 24

THE SYMPTOM

I have been betrayed. How can I open up my heart again after the pain
I've endured?

THE DIAGNOSIS

"Sometimes the person you'd take a bullet for is standing behind the
trigger..."
—*Anonymous*

THE PRESCRIPTION

When Judas, who had betrayed him, saw that Jesus was condemned, he
was seized with remorse and returned the thirty pieces of silver to the
chief priests and the elders. "I have sinned," he said, "for I have betrayed
innocent blood."
"What is that to us?" they replied. "That's your responsibility."
Matthew 17:3-4

THE TREATMENT PLAN

Had I known it was going to be like this, then I wouldn't ever have signed
up for the journey of trusting people too quickly. If I can have a transparent
moment with you, I never liked surprises. If it is your goal to get a favorable
response or reaction out of me, you should inform me of your plan rather
than surprise me. When I became a leader, I quickly realized what I wanted
as an ideal wasn't my consistent reality. I learned that if it wasn't one thing,
it was another. Life began to blow up in my face, and more importantly,
some people I blindly trusted would eventually betray me.

I learned when you genuinely love people; you become a prime
candidate for betrayal. Betrayal can only happen if you love. The saddest
thing about being let down is that it never comes from your enemies. A
snake can't bite you if it is far away from you, and generally speaking, if it
is approaching, you can tell it by the sound of its hissing! Snakes don't hiss

anymore; they call you bae, bro, or a friend. Yes, life has a way of reminding us that we all suffer through betrayal, rejection, and even abandonment. You are not exempt.

Betrayal shouldn't surprise us or cause us to doubt that God will remain with us even when we can't feel His presence!

Life is not about who's real to your face; it's about who's real behind your back. You have to become honest with those who have betrayed you and say to them, "Stop asking me to trust you while I'm still coughing up water from the last time you let me drown." Yes, betrayal hurts, but go ahead, love anyhow! In the end, love trumps betrayal.

THE FOLLOW-UP

Dear Lord Jesus,
You comprehend the hurt I feel from broken trust. Thank you for
being consistent and constant love in my life. I praise You for never
leaving me nor forsaking me. Amen.

Friends

THE SYMPTOM

My friendships feel shallow and temporary.

THE DIAGNOSIS

Settling for relationships that are not mutually beneficial leads to toxicity and dysfunction.

THE PRESCRIPTION

Perfume and incense bring joy to the heart,
and the pleasantness of a friend
springs from their heartfelt advice.
Proverbs 27:9

THE TREATMENT PLAN

Most of us have many acquaintances but very few friends, and even some of our friends may prove unfriendly or even unfaithful. As a consequence, at best, we have given ourselves over to transactional relationships that only benefit us at the moment. They are not transformative.

We have settled for replacing authentic friendship with acquaintances because we have never been able to break through the surface of superficial connections. We are wondering why we feel empty on the inside, never to discover the full value of a friendship because we occupy ourselves with surface relationships, and our meaningless meandering insulates us.

There is a difference between an acquaintance and a friend! An acquaintance will only see your representative and will never take the risk to go deeper. An associate will never know all about you and still desire to be around you. An acquaintance only wishes to be connected to you because of what you do versus who you are.

An acquaintance won't be there when you need them. They will call you when they require something, but they never check on you to see how you are doing. Acquaintances are like shadows: they follow you in the sun but leave in the darkness. Do you want to know who your real friends are? Mess up and see who's still there. Acquaintances tell you what you want to hear, but real friends tell you what you need to know. Acquaintances ask if they can come over, but real friends tell you they're already at the door!

Friendship is not about who you have known the longest. It's about who came and never left your side. My advice to you is to redefine your inner circle by the time you invest in your friendships. Dr. Martin Luther King, Jr. said, "In the end, we will remember not the words of our enemies, but the silence of our friends."

THE FOLLOW-UP

Dear Holy Friend,

Thank you for the blessing of genuine bonds that hold us together through sorrow and laughter. Teach me to love others the way you first loved me. In Your Son's Name. Amen.

The Next Chapter

THE SYMPTOM

I am so weary. I am carrying a heavy load.

THE DIAGNOSIS

When you feel like giving up, you have forgotten why you started the journey in the first place!

THE PRESCRIPTION

Let us not become weary in doing good, for at the proper time we will reap a harvest if we do not give up.
Galatians 6:9

THE TREATMENT PLAN

One of the most exciting things about reading a brand new book is becoming absorbed in the content to see what is coming next. It is fascinating as you are learning new concepts and growing enriched with new theories and stories from the author. But sometimes during my reading time, I become fatigued from the content and get tired of the process. Finally, you've reached the end of the chapter, and your eyes may become weary from reading. Still, you choose not to give up because, in just a few words, you know a new chapter is about to begin.

Yes, the last chapter you read of your life's story, you were almost ready to throw in the towel and say *this book can wait*. However, something magical happens when you work past the heaviness. It almost like it doesn't matter what happened in the difficult previous section. There was gleeful anticipation of what you were about to experience in the next chapter.

My friend, I believe that this is the key to your story! Expectancy is the instrument that will move you to see what divine possibilities are waiting for you. There is a new career that is about to be unleashed, a unique relationship that is about to start, a new business that is about to launch. I want to encourage you that it doesn't matter what happens in your current chapter.

You may feel that it is too long, and you want to fast-forward to see what the end of this story will be. Hold on. Don't give up! You are a few sentences away from your new beginning! God is about to bless you beyond your wildest expectations. Celebrate and get excited about what God has in store for you in the brand new pages of your life to come. Don't give up because you must read the rest to see what is coming next. Peace.

THE FOLLOW-UP

Dear Creator,

Advance my cause, edit my mistakes, and cover my issues so that I may receive all that you have for me!

In the Name above every name, Amen.

Public Persona *Versus* Private Pain DAY 27

THE SYMPTOM

Other people's lives are so much better than mine. How can everyone else have it so together and I can't?

THE DIAGNOSIS

Often, what we see is not the full picture, but a glimpse of what is being portrayed by the narrator.

THE PRESCRIPTION

Surely the Sovereign Lord does nothing
without revealing his plan
to his servants the prophets.
Amos 3:7

THE TREATMENT PLAN

Behind some brilliant and beautiful people, there's is suffering. People often adore others' lives because of status, position, power, and perceived blessings. However, the reality is that we actually have no idea of who they are. We have fallen in love with an image without the privilege of real intimacy to really know them. They look good in the public eye, but they could very well be going through a personal hell. We see the public persona, but we don't know their private pain.

I remember my daughter, a few years ago, finding herself in turmoil almost to the point of depression. She felt her life wasn't blessed; she wasn't doing enough, and life wasn't that good. I was shocked because I know as a father, I have provided and given her the proper attention that only a father could give a daughter. I asked her this simple question: "Jael, where is all of this feeling and emotion coming from, and how did this happen?"

She immediately explained that when she looks at the lives of the peers she follows on social media, it makes her feel inadequate and messes with her self-esteem. She was comparing her life to filters and fake narratives without the privilege of seeing what existed on the other side of the camera. I reassured her that what she was seeing is not always the reality of that person; it is just what they are portraying. She later discovered I was honest with her, and it began to change the way she felt about what she saw.

Don't judge or compare your life to what you see on the exterior. You could be looking at a false idol of empty expectation. My word for you today is to become excited about what God is doing in *your* life and be authentic and transparent to your experience; this is the real blessing. God made you for a purpose, so learn to adore you. This is the best thing that could ever happen to you!

THE FOLLOW-UP

Dear Originator,

Thank you for making me an original and not carbon copy. Help me to see what you see in me and bless me to understand my gift that you designed me! In Jesus' Name, I pray. Amen.

Mastering the Right Things

THE SYMPTOM

I am not arrogant, just cocky because I know what I bring to table.

THE DIAGNOSIS

"A mistake that makes you humble is better than an achievement that makes you arrogant."
—*Anonymous*

THE PRESCRIPTION

For by the grace given me I say to every one of you: Do not think of yourself more highly than you ought, but rather think of yourself with sober judgment, in accordance with the faith God has distributed to each of you.
Romans 12:3

THE TREATMENT PLAN

A martial arts student was meeting with her master and teacher at a table to discuss her life and aspirations. She was excited about sharing what she had learned and the incredible advancement of skill level. The master sat at the table, and he offered his student some tea. They looked at each other with great respect and caution.

The student said to her master, "I've learned all you have to teach me about defending myself. I have mastered your offensive techniques as well. I want to learn one thing more now. Master, please teach me about the ways of God."

The room went silent; her master looked at her intently with a smile on his face. The student waited as she was wondering what lesson she would learn from her master. Sitting in silence, the master took the tea kettle and started pouring tea into the student's cup. Soon the cup was full and began to spill over onto the saucer. Not saying a word, the master continued to pour the tea until it spilled over onto the dish and then onto the floor.

She finally said in desperation to her master, "Stop, stop, please stop! The tea is spilling over and is wasting all over the place. The cup can't take any more." The master then looked at his student and said, "That is the lesson, my friend." She said, "I don't get it. What lesson?" "You wanted to learn the ways of God," he replied, "but it is not possible!" The student asked why as she began to wipe up the tea, and the master leaned over to her and said, "You are so full of yourself that there is no room in your life for God. You can't learn the ways of God until you learn to empty yourself." He picked up the teacup and poured out the rest of the tea. He said to her, "This cup is ready to be used."

What about you? Have you become so engulfed in life circumstances that you've lost your ability to hear and learn from God? It is time for you to empty yourself of whatever is keeping you at capacity. God is waiting to fill you again with His revelation and goodness.

THE FOLLOW-UP

Dear Master,

Instruct me to remove those things, persons, or places in my life that have caused me to lose you. Guide my life so that I can be filled again with your presence! In Your Name I pray. Amen.

Beyond the Mess

THE SYMPTOM

I feel like a failure. I can't get anything right.

THE DIAGNOSIS

It is not defeat itself that destroys you, but accepting the role of victim.

THE PRESCRIPTION

For everyone born of God overcomes the world. This is the victory that has overcome the world, even our faith.

1 John 5:4

THE TREATMENT PLAN

James had experienced a lousy day at work. It seemed like everything that could go wrong eventually did for him. A customer cursed him out when he attempted to resolve an issue within his department for a colleague. Before arriving to work, he got a flat tire that made him late by a half hour. His workday came to an end, finally, and on his way home he stopped to pick up takeout for his family. He pulled into the driveway, got out of the car, and grabbed his belongings. He went to another side of the car to pick up the takeout and proceeded up the stairs, relieved to be home after such a long day. As he took a step forward, his phone rang, which distracted him, and he completely missed the first step, and everything that he was carrying catapulted right in front of him. The drinks splattered all over the staircase, fries went flying, and the burgers rolled back onto the driveway. He laid there with food over his body, and he started to scream and shout, "This is a big mess!" And before he could get out his next phrase, his wife came and said, "Honey, it's okay. We will survive. You just have to move beyond the mess."

I have had these days, but I learned that this is not the moment that I give up. The lesson for you is that you were born to succeed and not designed to fail. I know failure is a part of life's makeup, but it can't define who you will become. Only God can define your purpose because He has the keys to your destiny!

There is so much more in you that hasn't come to the surface yet, and I want to encourage you to go hard and get what is rightfully yours. Think big and dream big! Stop worrying about those intimidating moments. Don't pay attention to those who are annoyed by your presence and critique your every move. The ones who say "you can't" and "you won't" are probably the ones scared that "you will"! Listen, I believe in you. I am convinced that you are next in line for your miracle, but it comes as a result of your reaching beyond the mess and claiming what God has for you!

THE FOLLOW-UP

Dear Lord Jesus,
Scrub defeat from my subconscious, clean away my past, and wash
the windows of my future so that I may live in victory! Amen.

Break the Cycle

THE SYMPTOM

I seem to run into the same problems over and over.

THE DIAGNOSIS

People fall into patterns that were formed out of hurt, and those patterns are never modified.

THE PRESCRIPTION

Not only so, but we also glory in our sufferings, because we know that suffering produces perseverance; perseverance, character; and character, hope.
Romans 5:3-4

THE TREATMENT PLAN

God has perfect timing. Never early. Never late. It takes a little patience and a whole lot of faith, but in the end, it's worth the wait! Know this well: with God, it's always worth the wait.

It is essential to understand that what you are coming out of is the end of a cycle and season for your testimony. And just because you have crossed over into a new season, new year, and a new moment, it doesn't mean the season you have been in has effectively come out of you! When the past is still present, we learn how to function in our malady without ever being delivered from the behavior that we had adopted in our history. I call this being dysfunctionally functional.

You desire something different and have worked hard to make life changes, but you are still haunted by what you have become. Let's be clear: there are no perfect people, perfect relationships, perfect churches, or perfect families. Those Stepford-like pods of people who never fight, are always neat, and are always smiling only live in the land of make-believe. Healthy people have arguments. It is not wrong to have some level of agitation in your life.

The issue is around whether you believe God for deliverance. Yes, going through things you never thought you'd go through will take you places you never thought you'd go to. Sometimes the hard stuff is there for you to learn how to grow through it. You must hurt to know, fall to rise, lose to gain—because life's greatest lessons teach us how to grow through the pain. However, some people do become products of their environment, clinging onto behavioral attributes that keep them dysfunctionally functional.

As a consequence, those situations leave you as a victim in the cycles of abuse that set you up for a spinning wheel of misery. It's dangerous to live dysfunctionally functional when your life and existence are cheapened by misuse that is no respecter of persons. This is why God is calling you to be the person who breaks the cycle. If you were judged, choose to understand. If you were rejected, choose acceptance. If you were shamed, choose compassion. Be the person you needed when you were hurting, not the person who hurt you. Vow to be better than what broke you! When you decide to be this person, that is when God steps in on time and never late!

THE FOLLOW-UP

Dear Architect of the Universe,

Plan my steps, trace my history, and track my progress so that I may be closer to you through the suffering I have endured. In Jesus' Name, Amen.

Be Grateful

THE SYMPTOM

I know I complain a lot, but what is there to be happy about?

THE DIAGNOSIS

When you spend time complaining, it drains the resource you need to change your situation.

THE PRESCRIPTION

I will give thanks to you, Lord, with all my heart;
I will tell of all your wonderful deeds.
Psalm 9:1

THE TREATMENT PLAN

You and I think of a million things to complain about in our lives. We could complain about the weather, the people we have to endure, the financial conditions of the economy, not having enough support, and this list could go on and on. See, it is easy to stand at the complaint counter with no forecast that things will change for you.

I am here to tell you that your complaining can do you more harm than good. Complaining about your predicament can place you into a mental prison with no way to escape. And honestly, often what we are complaining about in our lives is fleeting.

Stop putting primary energy into momentary misery. Stop wasting precious thoughts on what you can't change and have no control over. Changing your perspective of what you are facing is the remedy for your release. When you refocus your attention on what you have and how it can work, it provides a pause for you to be grateful.

For every reason to complain, I have ten reasons to be thankful. Yes, things might not be great in your life, but I guarantee you that they could be a lot worse. When you shift the lens of complaints to a glass of gratitude, your life will take on a whole new meaning and level of appreciation.

Be grateful that where you are right now is not where you are going, and it is undoubtedly not the place you have been. So, be thankful that you have made it to this place of gratitude in your life despite the difficulties! Pickles are not permanent, so celebrate where you are because God has already declared that this is all fleeting!

THE FOLLOW-UP

Dear Gracious and Wonderful Savior,

Thank you for blessing me with the gifts of life, health, and wealth. I am not talking about material wealth only, but the spiritual wealth that comes from You. In Your Name I pray, Amen.

Not Sufficient

THE SYMPTOM

I feel the need to be in control so things will happen as they need to. For their own good, I'll do what I have to do to make sure people fall in line.

THE DIAGNOSIS

When your motives are geared to manipulate and persuade people into following your lead, it will prove dangerous.

THE PRESCRIPTION

And I will ask the Father, and he will give you another advocate to help you and be with you forever...
John 14:16

THE TREATMENT PLAN

There are a lot of things that you can do within your strength. You can lose weight, you can start a business, you can start a family, and you can even change the color of your hair. There are, however, some assignments in life that you cannot carry out without the power of the Holy Spirit.

Ministry is one of those things. The Spirit comes as an answered prayer of the disciple from Jesus the Christ. The Spirit functions as the comforter and a divine support system to remind you that you are not alone in serving God's people.

The disciples of Jesus could not carry out their ministry assignment without the power and presence of the Holy Spirit. Had Jesus sent the disciples forth in shaping the church without the Holy Spirit, He would have doomed them to failure and proven himself to be a cruel teacher.

There is a lesson for us all to learn here: Don't try to convert, change, or transform somebody in your own strength—it will not work. You will only frustrate yourself and the situation even more! You can talk to some people until you are blue in the face, and it will not convert the heart or change their mind. The change happens when they encounter the presence and power of the Holy Spirit.

The supernatural ability to influence the behavior of others comes through the indwelling of the Holy Spirit. God can do more with them than you could ever imagine. It is the power and appearance of the Holy Spirit that makes serving easier and ministry possible.

THE FOLLOW-UP

Dear God,

Fill us with Your presence, saturate our hearts with Your power, and permeate us with Your love. In Jesus' Name, Amen.

THE SYMPTOM

I pretend to be a better person than I really am. The real me isn't good enough.

THE DIAGNOSIS

We want to be perfect disciples of Christ, but many people are turned off by what they perceive to be fake and often are not willing to give it a second chance.

THE PRESCRIPTION

For you were once darkness, but now you are light in the Lord. Live as children of light (for the fruit of the light consists in all goodness, righteousness, and truth) and find out what pleases the Lord. Have nothing to do with the fruitless deeds of darkness, but rather expose them. It is shameful even to mention what the disobedient do in secret. But everything exposed by the light becomes visible—and everything that is illuminated becomes a light.
Ephesians 5:8-13

THE TREATMENT PLAN

I was reading an article about a phenomenon that has plagued our community for years. This young woman had an infatuation with labels and fashion, so much so that she took a trip to Canal Street in New York where she could stock up on her favorite fake designer wares. A logo-printed Louis Vuitton bag, a nylon Prada, plastic Chanel earrings, and a pasted-on Burberry Scarf seemed like they would do the trick. When she returned to her humble abode ready for the world with a pretend Louis slung over her shoulder, her giant puffy coat from Walmart suddenly camouflaged, she looked like a fashionista.

One night while wearing it, she recalled overhearing a wealthy woman whisper to her friends, "Oh look, I have the same one." She was half scared of being found out, half happy she passed as someone who could afford a $2,500.00 bag. The paint chipped at the edges eventually, but that fake Louis lasted a few years. The Prada ripped at the seams, but she used safety pins to put it back together and, whenever she opened it, you could see them, shiny and pointy. She stabbed herself a few times when they came undone, but the drops of blood were "worth the logo," she said.

Fakes, which lack the craftsmanship the real things are revered for, come with the anxiety of being found out. And yet, they are enticing. Getting faux designer duds felt like cheating on a test and getting straight A's. They made her feel like she was a part of an elite club even though she didn't have the credentials.

She later testified that she didn't believe in herself, but she believed in the bag! She needed something to mask her fear, insecurity, and anxiety—the fakes temporarily fulfilled her needs. She wanted to be seen and yet unseen. She later realized that the designer labels only had power because she gave them power.

We live in a world where the reason people are turned off by the church is that some of us wear the faux of favor but have been found out as not possessing the authentic transformation of God. Yes, some have settled for wearing fake forgiveness, artificial authority, mock miracles, pretend praise, fraudulent fellowship, and bogus blessings.

As a result, the mission of the church is lost in translation, leaving people wanting and wondering where Jesus is in the midst of what we call church. When the representatives of God's church lack the ability to offer loving relationships and leave seekers empty without the genuine fellowship of the church, they leave frustrated and defeated. When this happens, we have settled for the knock-offs!

I believe people are discovering that the appearance of authenticity isn't always reality. Sometimes it's the exact opposite. We must learn who is gold and who is simply gold-plated.

One of the hardest things to do in life is letting go of what you thought was real! The Good News is that Jesus is still showing up in your church as the genuine article. Therefore, you shouldn't let anything keep you from worshipping Him. When you worship the Lord, it empowers you to see His real presence operating in your life.

THE FOLLOW-UP

Dear Lord,

Remove anybody from my life who means me harm, serves no useful purpose, and is not genuine and dependable. Bless me with the insight to discern what is fake and give me the strength to let go and not look back!

The Secret to Elevation

THE SYMPTOM

I want my life to go to the next level, but I am also afraid to lose my current comfort.

THE DIAGNOSIS

Many individuals are not ready to make the sacrifices necessary to advance their lives.

THE PRESCRIPTION

The Lord, our God, said to us at Horeb, "You have stayed long enough at this mountain. Break camp and advance into the hill country of the Amorites; go to all the neighboring peoples in the Arabah, in the mountains, in the western foothills, in the Negev and along the coast, to the land of the Canaanites and to Lebanon, as far as the great river, the Euphrates. See, I have given you this land. Go in and take possession of the land the Lord swore he would give to your fathers—to Abraham, Isaac, and Jacob—and to their descendants after them."

Deuteronomy 1:6-8

THE TREATMENT PLAN

In this period of your life, God is getting ready to grow you in ways that you cannot yet imagine! I am so excited for you as I know with His mercy, your life is about to be better than good. God has placed within you the formula for favor. And because of His unmerited grace, you are ready to grow. You are hungry for it! You are passionate about it! You can see it, and you can taste it!

However, it will not come without a cost. It's been said that "Your elevation may require your isolation." You have circled in place for a while, and life has plateaued for you. Moving from the point you are to the new place God has promised will require you to experience some separation during the transition. This means that you will have to leave some friends, old behaviors, and habits behind so that you will be ready to receive the increase. Isolation is not designed as a punishment, but a blessing to demonstrate that you can make it on your own and can be independent. Please understand that this new level will not be without some trials. Some people refuse to cut ties with their history and as a consequence forfeit their destiny. Simply stated, some people cannot live with the idea that this is a season in their life when they will have to be alone. Every new level of blessings will come with its rounds of testing! You have to be determined that you are ready for what lies ahead for your future.

Are you prepared to be blessed? At this level, you must understand that the very thing that is going to elevate you can be the same thing that will challenge you. The secret of elevation is learning how to use the challenge to make yourself a champion instead of letting the trials use you. If you do that, you're in control of your life. If you don't, life controls you. Go ahead and advance, it's already yours!

THE FOLLOW-UP

Dear Father God,

Upgrade my passion, intensify my dreams, and enhance my hunger to be the best version of me that You desire for me to be! Amen.

You Have to Put in the Work

THE SYMPTOM

I want good things for my life, but I'm not sure what to do to bring them about. So I'm just waiting.

THE DIAGNOSIS

When you are uninspired to do what is necessary, it can make you miss out on what is essential.

THE PRESCRIPTION

Whatever you do, work at it with all your heart, as working for the Lord, not for human masters...
Colossians 3:23

THE TREATMENT PLAN

I was having a conversation with a close friend of mine, and he made this statement that blew me out of the water. He said, "I cannot watch you work out and expect myself to become healthy!" This statement is so true when it comes to many aspects of life. Working out is a metaphor for life, and it is not only about the calories you burn but also the progress you make. It is also how you deal with the tests that come your way.

While weight training is hard physically, the hardest part is the weight that you must push past in your mind. When you start your workout, there are so many reps during which you wonder how you are going to make it happen. You want to be done before you even start. When your hands are getting blisters, and your arms are beginning to burn, and your legs are becoming fatigued, and you know you have more to do, you start to convince yourself that this is not worth it. But then something within you challenges you to keep going and not give up, and that makes the difference.

It is about discovering how to push past your mental limitations and endure until you can see the results. You know no one can become what they are designed to be if they don't put in the work. Yes, it will become uncomfortable at times, but keep showing up and put in the work. Watching someone else sweating and struggling to push the weight off their chest may be useful for learning technique, but it will not change your physique. Discipline and consistency are a must, no matter what your goal.

I want to encourage you, my beloved, to pull up a bench for yourself and start pumping your iron. No pain, no gain! When the workout is over, those who put in the work will see the results they have always wanted.

THE FOLLOW-UP

Dear Jehovah God,

Formulate my appetite for execution, build my stamina, and develop my spirit to reach for excellence! Amen.

Closed Doors and Open Blessings

THE SYMPTOM

I've been rejected, and I don't know how to move on.

THE DIAGNOSIS

Most individuals cannot handle the rejection that comes their way, so they find other ways to receive the acceptance that they never got.

THE PRESCRIPTION

"To the angel of the church in Philadelphia write:
These are the words of him who is holy and true, who holds the key of David. What he opens no one can shut, and what he shuts no one can open. I know your deeds. See, I have placed before you an open door that no one can shut. I know that you have little strength, yet you have kept my word and have not denied my name.
Revelation 3:7-8

THE TREATMENT PLAN

You just experienced one door closing in your life, and it has left you devastated beyond your imagination. The rejection you feel is real and undeniable. It is enough to make you quit. I want you to understand that this moment is not the end of your story, and it is a defining turning point in your life.

I have some good news for you: there will be another door that will open up for you. Don't miss seeing the new door that God has opened for you because you spent so much time looking back at the door that has already closed. Not every plan works out. There will be failures and disasters. We don't have control over these things that happen, but we can command our perspective regarding these things. Please understand something, Beloved: the moment you heard the door slam, it was your sign that it's time to pay attention to what is about to open up for you! Build some inner peace with the truth that the door closed for a reason. Become aware of your thoughts and actions! Do they support the newness that you are about to obtain? Don't keep looking back when God is nudging you to look forward! Get ready to walk through that new door, because God has opened it just for you.

THE FOLLOW-UP

Dear Center of My Joy,

Help me visualize my future, correct my need to look back, and change my attitude toward my new beginning! In Jesus' Name, Amen.

● ●

A Reason to Smile

THE SYMPTOM

I wish things were different and that my life had gone the way I wanted.

THE DIAGNOSIS

"Stop looking for happiness in the same place you lost it!"
—*Anonymous*

THE PRESCRIPTION

A happy heart makes the face cheerful,
but heartache crushes the spirit.
Proverbs 15:13

THE TREATMENT PLAN

When you focus on what you don't have and what has gone wrong in your life, it can rob you of the joy of your potential. If you continue to allow a flawed focus to blind your revelation, you will never see all of the beautiful things that are happening in your life. Sure, you may have lost your house, but you still have shelter. Sure, you have made some mistakes, but you have the grace to begin again. Yes, the relationship ended unexpectedly, but you have love in your life. Isn't it great that you have peace of mind and the forgiveness to start all over again?

What has happened in your past cannot be undone. Hindsight is always 20/20, and if you could, you would ask life to give you another chance to do it all over again. However, the reality is that time is not fashioned for you to go back to your past and rearrange, anything because it could alter your destiny. So, please understand friends: you can never go back and make a brand new start, you can start at this moment now and make a brand new ending.

Your future is so bright, and the possibilities are limitless, so seize the moment of Now and start walking toward your glorious conclusion. Take control of your destiny and create a new you. I believe with you that the rest of your days shall be the best of your days. When life gives you a hundred reasons to cry, show the world that you have a thousand reasons to smile. Smiling relieves stress. Smiling elevates your mood by sending positive messages to your brain. Smiling lowers your blood pressure. Smiling helps your brain remain positive until your feelings follow suit.

THE FOLLOW-UP

Dear Gracious God,

Center my feelings, collect my attitude, and combine Your grace and mercy in my life so that I have multiple reasons to smile again. Amen.

Adjustments

THE SYMPTOM

I lack clarity and purpose. I feel overwhelmed and without direction.

THE DIAGNOSIS

Blurred vision causes poor focus and grave decisions.

THE PRESCRIPTION

So let's keep focused on that goal, those of us who want everything God has for us. If any of you have something else in mind, something less than total commitment, God will clear your blurred vision—you'll see it yet! Now that we're on the right track, let's stay on it.

Philippians 3:15-16

Peterson, E. H. (2005). *The Message: The Bible in Contemporary Language.* Colorado Springs, CO: NavPress.

THE TREATMENT PLAN

One thing I began to discover after turning forty over six years ago was that my vision started to shift. I previously had the option of wearing glasses for style and reading, but something changed as I began to grow older. I discovered that what I used to see became blurred, and I could no longer recognize what I was trying to perceive. Lines became fuzzy, and objects became obscure.

I met with an eye doctor, and she said it was time for me to get some progressive lenses. She shared that reason I was losing focus was that the lens inside the eye becomes less flexible the older you become.

This flexibility allows the eye to change focus from objects that are far away to those up close. When you lose flexibility, you need another lens to help refocus on what you used to be able to see. You might not need progressives or bifocals, but for many, life has caused us to become less flexible. And when you can't shift your focus according to the season that you are in, you need another lens that can help you deal with blurriness that life will bring. It doesn't matter whether or not you are nearsighted, farsighted, have astigmatism, or have 20/20 vision; blurry vision can be a symptom of more severe problems.

When you are going through hell and can't see your way through? That's blurry vision. When chaos becomes a constant companion in your life? Blurry vision. When confusion begins to know you on a first-name basis, you know your vision is being blurred. Of course, it is not just in your house—blurriness can happen to anyone. The severe underlying problem is in your inability to be self-aware.

Yes, life gets blurry when you are so overwhelmed that you are just functioning to get by and not living your best life. You are mentally shut down, failing to produce your best, or you are paralyzed and don't know where to begin. You can't see your way through the madness of unrealistic expectations. When life gets blurry, you have to adjust your focus. When you adjust your focus, God will clear your blurred vision! The moment you stop straining to see your purpose is the moment that you began to regain your vision!

Francis of Assisi said,

"Start by doing what's necessary, then do what's possible; and suddenly, you are doing the impossible."

THE FOLLOW-UP

Dear Great Jehovah,

Do what is necessary in my life to create a new experience so that I can see as far as You would allow me to go! Amen.

In the Meantime

THE SYMPTOM

The answer I need hasn't come. I feel like giving up.

THE DIAGNOSIS

Don't let life discourage you—everyone got where they are by beginning where they were.

THE PRESCRIPTION

The word of God to my Lord:
"Sit alongside me here on my throne
until I make your enemies a stool for your feet."
Psalm 110:1

THE TREATMENT PLAN

I want to encourage you today that everything the Lord has promised you shall come to pass! Please understand the promise is the affirmation that God gives to believers so that we can live by faith while we wait for the Lord to work on our behalf. Frequently, whatever God has promised us does not always work within our guidelines and timetables!

This reality is what makes His promises for us hard to deal with and understand. It is difficult for us to wait between the sign and the answer, especially when the season starts to become rough. Remember this: our faith is in God! God sets the timetable and doesn't follow the one you constructed within your expectations. God knows what He promised. He can't lie, He won't forget, and God always comes through for those who trust in Him.

By faith, we know it will happen in its appointed time, but what do you do in the meantime? The meantime is the waiting period between your promise declared and the answer received. The waiting period can be especially frustrating if you are going through this for the first time in your life.

While waiting on God, haters will rise in your life to discourage you and distract you from receiving your blessings. Don't get distracted by what is spoken against your coming truth. You know what God has said concerning your life, and God has a track record of delivering on His promises.

I want you to know that while you are in between the declaration and the promise, God will always handle your haters! Your goal is not to focus on them but to worship Him, and He will deal with them on your behalf. This is time for you to get some rest and know that, in the end, it will work out just the way He planned it for you! God will make your enemies your footstool!

THE FOLLOW-UP

Dear Lord,

Drive my process, press my claim, and manifest my promises for your glory! In Jesus' Name, Amen.

Out of Bounds

THE SYMPTOM

I'm tired of waiting for God's plan. I'm about to take matters into my own hands.

THE DIAGNOSIS

"We cut him off, and there was nowhere for him to go but out of bounds... It's still the greatest move I've ever seen in basketball, the all-time greatest."

—*Magic Johnson*

THE PRESCRIPTION

"Have I not commanded you? Be strong and courageous. Do not be afraid; do not be discouraged, for the Lord, your God will be with you wherever you go."

Joshua 1:9

THE TREATMENT PLAN

Recently, I was amazed at the beginning of the documentary *The Last Dance* featuring the story of the Chicago Bulls NBA team. It renewed my love for basketball, and at the same time it made me miss the game as the entire NBA season has been postponed indefinitely in the year 2020 amid the raging COVID-19 pandemic.

The documentary made me reminisce of the Chicago Bulls dynasty and how the game has evolved. As much as the game has developed over the years, there is one thing for sure that hasn't changed: You can't play the game if your teammate is holding the ball out of bounds. You can debate whether or not Michael Jordan is the greatest of all time (he is!). You can debate whether or not Dennis Rodman was as much a distraction as he was an asset to the Chicago Bulls dynasty. But one thing is for sure: You can't play the game if the ball is out of bounds. That's why over and over you have seen players leaping across sports analysts and commentators in attempts to keep the ball inbounds. In fact, Rodman was notorious for falling out of bounds and he even got in trouble for kicking a camera man while falling out of bounds, but he always made sure the ball was in!

He was the kind of player that tried his best to save the ball even if it meant that he got hurt in the process. This is a life lesson we can learn from the game: In life, we are at our best and have the best odds of winning if we are inbounds. When you try to continue to play the game when the ball is out of bounds, it leads to a turnover and potentially a loss. We try to hold on to the ball because we are afraid that if our opponent gets a hold of it, we might lose the lead we worked so hard to build.

I don't know what ball you are dribbling while trying to stay in the game. It might be your career, your family, your small or grown children, or your finances. You must stay on the court of life to have a fighting chance to win the game! However, I will guarantee that you will not succeed if you are out of bounds. This lesson applies to our walk with God. When we are wandering outside of the will of God, we are subject to grief, disappointment, and heartache with no one to depend on. Sometimes these same issues can happen inside God's will, but there is no guarantee that you will have the support you need to gain victory. There's no need for a coach when you are out of bounds of His grace. If you are out of bounds, I recommend you call for a time out, reset the clock and get ready to play! You can do it!

THE FOLLOW-UP

Dear Divine Coach,

Show me how to keep my balance, maintain my agility, and stay graceful while remaining inbounds. I know I can win if I stay in the game! Amen.

Stop and Breathe!

THE SYMPTOM

Sometimes I feel like my anger takes over. I struggle to maintain control of my rage.

THE DIAGNOSIS

When you're upset and frustrated, never trust your feelings in the moment. They can lead you down some treacherous roads.

THE PRESCRIPTION

For his anger lasts only a moment,
but his favor lasts a lifetime;
weeping may stay for the night,
but rejoicing comes in the morning.
Psalm 30:5

THE TREATMENT PLAN

Silence is violence. This is a phrase that I have added to my arsenal of principles I attempt to live my life by. The longer you do not address something that has annoyed you and has caused you to become offended, the higher the chance your response will become disruptive to your livelihood and possibly even violent. As a consequence, you execute firm decisions based on volatile emotions. This kind of decision making is never sufficient for you because it sets you up for failure.

Even when you are convinced that you are absolutely right and justified, it doesn't give you the power or excuse to create more harm to those around you. Allow me to offer you some advice when this is happening. Stop. Breathe. Give yourself time and space. Work on you. Respond consciously instead of impulsively. Talk about it. Keep your mind open. Be willing to open your eyes and see through the lenses of others. Be kind to yourself. Be willing to change. Be ready to ask for assistance. Be prepared to let go of those who are doing more harm than good with their version of "helping."

It's one thing to get validation from people around you to fuel your justified sense of self, but it's another thing to find friends who are going to be straight with you and help you fix the problem and yourself along the way. It is imperative to create boundaries to prevent the infiltration of toxicity. Toxic people permanently stain those who are around them. Stand up for yourself, but don't forget to stand up for the ones around you, too. Believe it or not, they may feel like your worst enemy right now—but they can become your ally the moment you stop being your own worst enemy.

Please wait. Work on yourself, hone your reactions, and pick up some coping abilities while you are at it. Living and dwelling inside your head and closing everyone off makes your thoughts angrier. Learn to talk about it. Sometimes time will open your eyes if you keep your mind open in the process. These adverse results don't have to be your reality!

THE FOLLOW-UP
Dear Eternal God,
Operate on my heart, work on my grace, and control my tongue that I may not misrepresent you! Amen.

Is Someone on the Line?

THE SYMPTOM

I want to believe, but it is hard to trust when people are so inconsistent.

THE DIAGNOSIS

Lack of commitment changes the dynamics of a relationship in a heartbeat.

THE PRESCRIPTION

Commit to the Lord whatever you do,
and he will establish your plans.

Proverbs 16:3

THE TREATMENT PLAN

I am always fascinated by the random memories that I have from mundane childhood moments that turn out to become life treasures. One moment in particular, I remember, was the novel experience of talking on the phone. This was a time not that long ago before smartphones, Zoom, and social media. We were all blown away by the idea that someone else could be on another end of the line who was so far away but talking to you as if they were in the same room.

The anticipation grew in her eyes when my grandmother would get the chance to speak to our distant relatives in other parts of the country using the telephone. The talks weren't filled with a lot of rhetoric, but the idea that she could connect in this way amazed her to no end. She loved the idea of talking on the phone because she could guarantee that there would be somebody who would talk back to her on the other side.

The very next Christmas came and a cousin of mine who was four years old received a Fisher-Price Classic Chatter phone. You know the one: it was the rolling toy telephone with eyes and a big smile that so many children of the time owned. My cousin played with the toy for a while, but she eventually got mad and would push the phone away after she would say hello and receive no reply. She would sob and tell everybody "There is nobody here."

She didn't want to play with the phone because she knew that nobody was holding the receiver on the other end. My cousin learned a valuable lesson that day on Christmas morning, and her childhood revelation also applies to real adult relationships. A relationship with zero trust is like having a phone with no service: you are just playing games. I want to encourage you that if this is your story, please hang up the phone and place your call again on a real phone!

THE FOLLOW-UP

Dear Alpha and Omega,

Connect my life with someone who appreciates me, join my heart to that which promotes my health, and attach my desires to someone who loves, respects, and commits to you and me! Amen.

It Matters

THE SYMPTOM

It doesn't matter what other people think about me. God knows who I am, and that's all that matters.

THE DIAGNOSIS

When you're not self-aware, it will set you up to experience loss of influence due to a bad reputation.

THE PRESCRIPTION

A good name is more desirable than great riches;
to be esteemed is better than silver or gold.

Proverbs 22:1

THE TREATMENT PLAN

There is a declaration that I know you're familiar with. You have often heard it, and I myself have made this same statement foolishly many times: "I don't care what people think about me!"

This narrative might hold weight if you are not trying to make an impact on life or leave a legacy behind. This affirmation might be reality if you are someone who doesn't care about how your life will affect others. One anonymous writer states that, "A person's reputation is a mixture of what his friends, enemies, and relatives say behind his back." You have a reputation. Are you aware of it?

If the truth is told, we seldom reflect to consider what others might think when the context is right because we're assured that our status within our circles is unaffected. And adversarial judgments held by those outsides of our social networks may have less weight than others because they are less likely to influence future relationships. Is it only when our reputation is threatened that we begin to wonder what people are going to think?

The fact is that it matters what people think of you! I know this might not be a revelation for you, but it is a truth worth exploring. Most of the time, we say things like, "I don't care what people think," out of the scars of critique and contempt when people judge and don't know you. And, indeed, in such cases you shouldn't care what they think! But in the case of your legacy, it really matters what people think about you. The picture you paint with your life can stain someone's view of you, or it may be the sunshine they needed to make it through a tough time. So, I encourage you to pay close attention to the impression that you leave behind, because it is important whether you care or not!

THE FOLLOW-UP

Dear Gracious and Loving God,

Permit me to care about my life, my reputation, and my character

that I may honor You by how I love, live, and learn. Amen.

I Want It Now

THE SYMPTOM

I hate waiting. I get antsy and restless when things don't happen fast enough.

THE DIAGNOSIS

Many people rush into situations that could have caused them less damage if they had just patiently waited.

THE PRESCRIPTION

Take delight in the Lord,
and he will give you the desires of your heart.

Psalm 37:4

THE TREATMENT PLAN

Have you been bitten by the bug of "I've got to have it now"? I don't know about you, but most people want what they want now and not later. Please don't be hard on yourself when you hear this fact! We are all conditioned from the very start to want more, and you discover at an early age how to get it. As a newborn, you cry because you want food; and as a toddler, you cry because you didn't get what you wanted and you continue to cry until someone paid you attention.

Kids make out lists of what they want for the holidays. When we get to go to college or graduate from high school, we have a wishlist on shopping sites so people can get us exactly what we want before the next phase of life. You might have created a gift registry at department stores when you set up home with your partner.

Our culture runs on want, and it's why so many people are unhappy. The media tells us we're supposed to want to drive this car, wear these clothes, listen to this music, or look like this celebrity—and if you don't, then you're some outcast.

Want has become so much a part of our natural language that it's contributing to our downfall. You might even tell the waitstaff, "I want coffee," rather than perhaps saying, "I'd like coffee." Same message, but the alternative wording creates such different energy! And our demands can create such stress when things don't go our way.

Yes, when it doesn't happen the way we want, we are tempted to ask, "When, God, when?" Our "When?" questions really don't have anything to do with God, but everything to do with our wants. When you confuse your want with your when, you are setting yourself up for failure and frustration. You run the risk of jeopardizing God's plan for your life as you race time to satisfy your wants when you haven't prepared for your when! Timing is everything, so trust the process!

THE FOLLOW-UP

Dear Great Sustainer of Life,

Caution my moves, advise my paths, and inform my wants so that I may win in the end. Amen.

Misguided Mayhem

THE SYMPTOM

I feel if you got a chance to know me, then maybe you wouldn't judge by a few misguided actions.

THE DIAGNOSIS

You may be good, but when the bad leads you, no one ever gets to see your good because it has been colored by the bad.

THE PRESCRIPTION

But because of his great love for us, God, who is rich in mercy, made us alive with Christ even when we were dead in transgressions—it is by grace you have been saved.
Ephesians 2:4-5

THE TREATMENT PLAN

I wanted to share a personal story in this devotional that I am not proud of and is still embarrassing until this day. I have learned that it is okay that you have some dark moments in your past, as they help you appreciate the light God has given you. Years ago, in my pre-teens, before I accepted Jesus Christ as my Lord and Savior, I got into some crazy trouble.

Now, don't judge me, because you don't have the privilege of telling me what you've done. Okay, so here's' what happened. I will never forget that day as it was in the dead of winter, and the warm breath from my lungs was visible as it met the biting cold.

A few of my so-called friends decided that we would take some opaque Christmas light bulbs off of a string of lights that was connected to an outside tree and catapult them off into some random person's house. It sounded like a gunshot that exploded onto the brick wall of this person's home. We disconnected the light bulbs one by one and used that brick wall for target practice.

We thought it was funny as we walked away from the scene, looking to see what else we could get into for that evening. Things were okay until the police came, and we all ran. I ran straight scared and didn't know what else to do, but eventually I was the one they caught. I was placed into the squad car by the cop, and the officer began to berate me about bad behavior, but I was too young to go straight to jail and had the choice to be taken to my mother or father. The officer asked me which I would prefer, and a pregnant pause came over me. I felt like I was choosing between being taken to heaven (my father) or hell (my mother and her formidable punishment record). I decided on my father. He was working at one of his restaurants nearby, and I had to ride past while my so-called friends watched me constrained to the backseat of a squad car, I was marked, and my fate didn't look good.

I finally arrived with fear on my mind and panic in my heart. The officer asked my father whether he wanted to handle me or have me taken into the station. My father hesitated and then said to the officer, "I will take care of him for sure!"

I started to think I made the wrong choice. And then my father said to the officer, "Thank you for the option, but you can't do what I can do because I am his father." And with that, I was released into the hands of my father. That night, I knew I was headed for punishment, but the whole night went past without my father laying a hand on me. I expected my father to whip me for my actions. (Keep in mind this was in the early '80s and before "time outs" became the preferred method of discipline.) That night my father never laid a hand on me. He continued to strike the grill with his spatula as he cooked for customers. He questioned me the entire time about why I would put myself in that predicament, but my father never laid one finger on me as a consequence of his marathon talk we had that night. This was my worst punishment ever, anticipating a whipping that never happened. My next blessing was that the officer who threatened to punish me could not touch me, because I was in the hands of my father!

This is the lesson that I share with you that even in your mess, God still gives you mercy! Mercy means that you deserve the punishment, but instead, you receive compassion. Justice demanded that I should've been punished for the rest of the year, but Mercy said to give me another chance! We all have messed up at some point, but God's mercy is still working on your behalf.

THE FOLLOW-UP

Dear God of Mercy,

Rescue me from irresponsibility, redeem my path, restore my life
so that I may carry out my calling to do your will. In Jesus' Name,
Amen.

It is Not That Serious

THE SYMPTOM

I avoid confrontation because I don't like to deal with the emotion of it all.

THE DIAGNOSIS

Too many people allow their emotions to determine how their stories will play out. When this happens, you are already defeated.

THE PRESCRIPTION

A gentle answer turns away wrath,
but a harsh word stirs up anger.
Proverbs 15:1

THE TREATMENT PLAN

There are a lot of reasons that I am grateful to have had my father in my life as long as I did. He was a good, hardworking man who was often misunderstood. However, my father taught me precious lessons about life that I would like to share with you! He admonished me that if I ever found myself in a situation that was getting ready to turn quickly into a battle, walk away. My father said to me, "Understand Son, whatever it is, know it is not worth your losing your integrity." He also taught me that if I was in an awkward conversation with someone and they raised their voice to me, I should lower mine. It didn't matter who the person may be, a friend, a spouse, a child, or even a parent. He looked me in the eye and said, "You know what the Bible says: 'A soft answer turns away wrath.'" He realized that a gentle response demonstrates sensitivity and compassion, and it is accomplished by patience and precision. When you respond harshly, it conjures up negativity that you can't control.

He desired for me to understand that he was not suggesting avoiding confrontation at all. He recognized instinctively that there are some circumstances where and when you must confront the issue and not the person. But we must be very cautious with people who are always looking for a fight. Most of the time, they have nothing to lose. The argument they push has nothing to do with you, but a battle that they have within themselves. Give them space and time to work out what they are wrestling with, and in the meantime, you choose the kind approach. Remember, it takes two for a fight.

THE FOLLOW-UP

Dear God,

Arrest my thoughts, hold my tongue, and capture my consciousness, so that I may be able to bless You and others! In Jesus' Name, Amen.

Keep Moving

THE SYMPTOM

I am not sure I can keep going. I feel like giving up.

THE DIAGNOSIS

Many individuals give up after going through a traumatic experience, never really recovering from what had happened to them.

THE PRESCRIPTION

The Lord makes firm the steps
of the one who delights in him;
though he may stumble, he will not fall,
for the Lord upholds him with his hand.
I was young, and now I am old,
yet I have never seen the righteous forsaken
or their children begging bread.
Psalm 37:23-25

THE TREATMENT PLAN

When I was growing up, we didn't have smartphones or access to many of the digital platforms we use today. We had to use our imagination to play a lot of games. When I was a little boy, many of my friends had Hot Wheels cars that we played with, and we would smash the cars into each other to see which car was strongest among them. I would watch my friends play, because my cars couldn't stand up to their rough game. Until one day, when my mother got me a Tonka Mighty Dump Truck.

My Tonka Mighty Dump Truck was unique because it was made of cast iron steel, with a yellow paint job as if it was a real vehicle. My dump truck would destroy those little cars. So, while we were playing, one of my friends got jealous of me winning all of the battles. He took a hammer and hit the side of my Tonka truck. My eyes were wide as the hammer slammed into the side of my Tonka. I was horrified!

I thought my Tonka Dump Truck was done, and my friend said, "Now let's see what your Tonka can do!" I looked at the side of the truck. I was petrified! I thought my favorite toy would be destroyed if it endured any more abuse. I said to myself, "It's over!" I picked up the truck to look at the damage and decided to give it one more roll. I turned that truck on its four wheels, and my Tonka rolled like it was never hit. It had a dent in it, but it kept on moving! It was made of quality materials.

Life may have knocked the wind out of you. You may be startled by the blow and you may have begun to believe that this is the end of your journey. But I challenge you to give life one more try! You're made of tough stuff. God designed you to take a hit and keep on rolling! Life may have damaged you, but it hasn't destroyed you. Here is the blessing: Damaged people are dangerous because they know that they can endure. My advice to you? Keep on rolling!

THE FOLLOW-UP

Dear Father,

Perfect my portion, rectify my life, and improve my opportunities so that I will have the power I need to endure! Amen.

Staying on Top

THE SYMPTOM

I am under so much pressure. I'm not sure I can handle it all.

THE DIAGNOSIS

Many people don't have the tools to cope when life becomes nasty, and they give up prematurely as a result of their circumstances.

THE PRESCRIPTION

David praised the Lord in the presence of the whole assembly, saying, "Praise be to you, Lord,
the God of our father Israel,
from everlasting to everlasting.
Yours, Lord, is the greatness and the power
and the glory and the majesty and the splendor,
for everything in heaven and earth is yours.
Yours, Lord, is the kingdom;
you are exalted as head over all.
Wealth and honor come from you;
you are the ruler of all things.
In your hands are strength and power
to exalt and give strength to all.
Now, our God, we give you thanks,
and praise your glorious name.
1 Chronicles 29:10-13

THE TREATMENT PLAN

Instead of going to pieces under pressure, you have to learn how to stay on top through prayer! One of my favorite characters in the biblical narrative is King David. David had humble beginnings, and because of God's favor, he was exalted amid conflict and crisis. He is not my favorite because of his lifestyle or the status that he achieved at the pinnacle of life;

David is my favorite character in the Bible because of his prayer life. He was a man of prayer, and he knew how to get to the divine ear of God.

I believe on more than one occasion that the Lord heard David's prayer. Yes, when life got rough for David, and when those he led in his army wanted to end his life, he didn't retaliate; he went to God in prayer! Prayer is the lesson that I have learned from his character.

When life gets tough, you need to go straight to the source that can give you strength in times of need. When life is unfair, you can go to God and tell Him about every one of your troubles. When things grow worse in our lives, there is a tendency for us to retreat into our silos, not realizing this is the time that we need God the most.

When you are walking and living out this faith journey, you must anticipate that things will not always be easy. You will experience some trials and tribulations that will make you want to quit the course of faith. You didn't study this hard just to walk out on the test. You didn't go through all of this pain just to become a drop out of the faith. You didn't complete the next level of your development just to quit before you can walk across the stage of victory. Don't pay the tuition and fail to get the diploma! How do you sustain yourself when life gets hard? You can stay the course through prayer. Prayer fuels your trust to believe that, despite how painful your experience will become, you can make it!

THE FOLLOW-UP

Dear Jehovah Nissi,

You continue to wave the banner of victory over my life! Continue to set the standard through prayer, and I bless You forever! Amen.

I Want More!

THE SYMPTOM

I want to do better, but more stuff keeps being piled upon my plate and it is hard to manage all of the priorities.

THE DIAGNOSIS

Mismanagement of priorities will often lead to an unfulfilled life.

THE PRESCRIPTION

But seek first his kingdom and his righteousness, and all these things will be given to you as well.
Matthew 6:33

THE TREATMENT PLAN

Recently, I couldn't help but overhear a nearby conversation between two individuals who were in a relationship. The couple was discussing their priorities, needs, and goals; and as the conversation became more intense, one of them said something that made me think God was speaking to me.

He said to her, "If you want me in your life, put me there. I shouldn't be fighting for a spot." These words made me reflect on my relationship with God. Words shared between two lovers transcended a lover's quarrel to become a clarion call for me to reflect on my relationship with the One who first loved me. Often, we make space for everything and everybody except the One who blesses us over and over again.

It amazes me that it took me eavesdropping on a conversation that day to hear God's challenge to my relationship with Him. I must admit that I allow the busyness of schedules, deadlines, the demands of a growing church, and devotion to family lure me to forget the One who gives me the energy to be all things to all people. After working all day and spending a few moments with my family, I lay my head down. In that moment I realize that I haven't prayed intentionally and haven't spent any time in devotion to the Lord. The guilt slides into my mental space right next to my good intentions, and before I know it, the fatigue has won for the evening! I am fast asleep, and I am starting the day all over again.

So, this was a conversation that I so needed to hear, because I know I can do better by God! What about you? Have you allowed the busyness of life to draw you into being busy, but not productive and fruitful? Maybe God is speaking to you right now: "If you want me in your life, put me there. I shouldn't be fighting for a spot." It is past time for us all to be intentional about spending some quality time with God so that we can hear His voice and listen to His directions for our lives. When we put him first, we will experience a supernatural joy that could only come through His amazing grace.

THE FOLLOW-UP

Dear Jehovah Tsidkenu,

We thank you for Your patience with us, Your tolerance of our forgetfulness, and Your understanding of our unfaithfulness. Give us the grace to draw closer to You intentionally! Amen.

Love Won't Let Me Wait

THE SYMPTOM

I am so weary of waiting for someone to love me.

THE DIAGNOSIS

Desperation can lead to poor choices when you are choosing a mate.

THE PRESCRIPTION

Love is patient, love is kind. It does not envy, it does not boast, it is not proud.

1 Corinthians 13:4

THE TREATMENT PLAN

Masingita Ringani says, "Don't rush to fall in love, because even in fairy tales, the happy ending takes place on the last page." I know somebody is saying "Oh, you are too late with the quote, because I am already experiencing the nightmare of my life." It is never too late. But you must take time to find one with whom you can not only experience a level of euphoric ecstasy, but also share goals and aspirations.

You definitely will not learn whether a person can adequately fill those roles by spending a couple of hours with them. A lasting relationship takes time to develop, and true love can't be discerned without the filter of time's passage. Love is much more than a feeling; it is a choice. And that choice transforms into a commitment that lasts beyond the moment and into something that can be rewarding. It's not how fast you fall in love that matters, but when you do fall in love, know that you have signed up for the bumps and bruises that come with being in a relationship. There is not a five-minute YouTube tutorial on how to be and remain in love. You will have to take the time to read the whole manual. Happy endings will come when you have successfully gone through the tests and trials of the beginning chapters of your relationship. So, don't rush to fall in love, but take your time to read the situation that you are in so that you won't have to reread what you might have missed the first time!

THE FOLLOW-UP

God of Love,

Impart to me the grace to see my possibilities, reveal my options, and show me my future so that I can experience the happiest ending ever! Amen.

Denied and Rejected

THE SYMPTOM

I just want to love and have that love returned. Instead, I feel like I've been thrown out like garbage.

THE DIAGNOSIS

When you feel rejection, it plants you in a dark place that you will either grow from or die from.

THE PRESCRIPTION

As you come to him, the living Stone—rejected by humans but chosen by God and precious to him—you also, like living stones, are being built into a spiritual house to be a holy priesthood, offering spiritual sacrifices acceptable to God through Jesus Christ.

1 Peter 2:4-5

THE TREATMENT PLAN

We all have some darkness in us. That darkness stems from the rejection that we've had to endure. You didn't start this way. You were a happy, bold, and positive person until refusal showed up at your address. People don't start out evil from the onset—pain can chip away at our humanity without our notice.

Rejection happened, and your life took a turn because of it. Yes, someone dismissed you when they should have embraced you; someone refused your advice when they could have listened, and you are now bitter because of it. Bitterness turns into darkness, and it is never good to try to navigate life in darkness—or when darkness is growing within you.

You will murder some relationships that could have survived; you will assassinate some characters that deserved more from you, and you will kill the potential that could have helped you along your journey. This happened all because you experienced some rejection. Allow me to hang out here, momentarily, to suggest that rejection doesn't mean you aren't good enough; *it means the other person failed to notice what you have to offer.*

Rejection is not proof that you lack value or talent. If you believe in what you have to offer, then don't stop offering it simply because someone can't appreciate it. Many people are not very good at recognizing value, but that doesn't mean you won't eventually find an audience that will. One writer says it like this: "Every time I thought I was being rejected from something good, I was being re-directed to something better." Hmm, that's good! When one window closes, another barn door opens wide. Jehovah God sees your worth and knows your value! God knows you are good enough, and He is planning something more rewarding, more fulfilling, and greater than you can imagine. It is now time for you to see what God has already seen in you from the moment you were created. Remember, the Hebrew people rejected Jesus. But their rejection didn't mean He wasn't good enough—they simply failed to see His worth. And you know His earthly story ends with despise and rejection, but He became the Savior of the world! This shows us that what people fail to notice about you might be your greatest gift!

THE FOLLOW-UP

Dear God of Mercy,

Rinse off the darkness that stains my life and soak me in Your grace that I may become more and more like You! In Your Son's Name, I pray. Amen.

Ready or Not!

THE SYMPTOM

I messed up pretty bad, and quite honestly I don't know how to handle it!

THE DIAGNOSIS

Errors are a part of life, but they become detrimental when we don't acknowledge mistakes for what they are.

THE PRESCRIPTION

If we claim to be without sin, we deceive ourselves, and the truth is not in us. If we confess our sins, he is faithful and just and will forgive us our sins and purify us from all unrighteousness. If we claim we have not sinned, we make him out to be a liar, and his word is not in us.
1 John 1:8-10

THE TREATMENT PLAN

Yep, we all make mistakes, but not all of us are ready to admit it because we are essentially ego-driven creatures. One reason we may not accept our errors is that we would rather avoid the consequences and often damage to relationships.

Although mistakes are often viewed in a negative light, I don't think all errors are bad things in our lives. While in meditation about my life, I read that "Mistakes in life are not meant to make us fail, but to see how far we can fly." Yes, that's right: to fly and soar above your errors and issues to a place that you have never experienced before. I believe some of the best lessons learned in life come from errors. I know it is a painful way to learn, but the things you've been through have helped form you into the man or woman that you are right now.

Making mistakes is part of being human. The key is becoming self-aware so that you can learn what went wrong and learn from it. It is also critical that you do not blame someone else for your mistakes or poor decisions. Having an honest conversation about why you are in this situation can lead to others wanting to help you make it through what you are experiencing. Seeing our errors and mistakes clearly makes room for great blessing; but if we can't see the breaks, flaws, or deficiencies in our behavior, we are forever confined to the same actions and limitations we've always had the opportunity to improve.

I know it's easier said than done. And, I also know it feels unpleasant to realize and admit that we've screwed something up. But sooner or later, we have to acknowledge it, accept it, and learn from it. Mistakes can change you for the better if you are willing to take some time to learn from them instead of hiding from them. They can become the wings you need to soar to the next level. Don't look down now because you are flying high above the mess you've just overcome.

THE FOLLOW-UP

Dear Jehovah Raah,

Thank you for guiding us to still waters; it is only You who can restore our souls and lead us to righteousness for Your Name's sake. Do it, Lord, for me! Amen.

Your Blessing in Disguise

THE SYMPTOM

I know something is growing inside of me that makes feel bitterness and rage. I don't know why they don't like me.

THE DIAGNOSIS

You can drive yourself crazy trying to figure out why someone else doesn't like you.

THE PRESCRIPTION

Do not repay evil with evil or insult with insult. On the contrary, repay evil with blessing, because to this you were called so that you may inherit a blessing.
1 Peter 3:9

THE TREATMENT PLAN

The adversity that you experienced from the haters maligning you was being used to bless you! But your attitude must change for you to see that it helped you. In every moment of hurt beneath the blow, there is always a place of blessing. You may not be able to see it while it is happening, but after some time has passed, you will begin to feel the benefit. Yes, God uses your enemies to bless you without their consent.

It has been said that no matter how good you are; there will always be someone who is going to be against you. You have to learn to live with the ambiguity that comes with excelling and encountering the favor of God. This is why you must never allow those who hate to limit your success. God didn't give you the strength to get back on your feet so that you could run back to the same thing that knocked you down! Be strong enough to stand alone, smart enough to know when you need help, and confident enough to ask for it.

You are designed to be a success, and with victory come critics. You must master who you are and stay focused on the purpose in which God has given you to live and impact the world. Remember, people only rain on your parade because they're jealous of your sun and tired of their shade. However, I want to encourage you to keep on shining, because somebody depends on your sunrays of hope to survive!

God has strategically positioned you to be an inspiration to those who feel like they can't make it. No pressure, but keep on shining because you are blessing those who watch how you handle your haters. Remember, you thought it was insulting you, but it was actually blessing you and releasing the anointing to flow into your life and onto others.

THE FOLLOW-UP

Dear El Roi,

You are the One who knows all, hears all, and sees all. Move me in the right direction despite the opposition that I may experience! Amen.

Contagion

THE SYMPTOM

Life feels so out of control right now. I don't know what to think or believe.

THE DIAGNOSIS

Disbelief becomes the rope that strangles our faith.

THE PRESCRIPTION

When you pass through the waters,
I will be with you;
and when you pass through the rivers,
they will not sweep over you.
When you walk through the fire,
you will not be burned;
the flames will not set you ablaze.
For I am the Lord your God,
the Holy One of Israel, your Savior.
Isaiah 43:2-3

THE TREATMENT PLAN

In 2011, a movie entitled *Contagion* was released. It was a realistic, sensational film about a global epidemic. It was being marketed as a thriller; a terrifying speculation about how a new airborne virus could enter the human species and spread relentlessly in very little time. This movie focused on trying to find a vaccine at the Center of Disease Control in Atlanta.

The setting in *Contagion* is a baffling one in which people defy isolation and reject the cure. This film by Steven Soderbergh is skillful at telling the story through the lives of several key characters and the casual interactions of many others. It makes it clear that people do not "give" one another a virus; a virus is a life form evolved to seek out new hosts—always one jump ahead of death as its carriers die off. All viruses originate somewhere, and in an age of air travel, they can reach a new continent in a day. We thought that this was a thriller made for theaters, but nine years later, we are dealing with our version of *Contagion*.

During early 2020, COVID-19 is the opposite of this make-believe virus. COVID-19 is not an airborne disease, but it is a virus that has left us baffled and disoriented. The coronavirus will forever change the way we see our world and our lives. We are confused by how something that seems so simple has left us in pandemonium and desperate for our lives to return to normalcy. Consequently, there is no way that our lives will be normal again. This pandemic is a pivotal moment in history.

It also offers us some valuable insight: when you become comfortable with the way things are, it will give you a false sense of security and a belief that you can control what happens around you. This virus is a brutal reminder that you were never in control, regardless of what you thought. As a consequence, God will allow divine disruptions to show up at the most inconvenient times to remind you that there is something bigger than you. I know you had accepted this as a reality before this moment. However, many of us were going about our lives business as usual with no expectation of real change, and change upended our world.

The life you were living has now been intruded upon and altered by something you thought wasn't real or even worth considering. What do you do when the world you have built is continuously shaken, and there is no end in sight? How do you handle it when your life comes to a screeching halt?

Let me encourage you: Your life will be okay! Don't stress yourself out with things you can't control or change. Things have changed. Times have changed. Situations have changed. Paths have changed. Your predictable future has changed. You have changed.

Sometimes you have to remind yourself that it'll be okay. Maybe not now, perhaps not tomorrow, but one day it will be okay! This understanding is where hope lives and faith reigns.

THE FOLLOW-UP

Dear Lord Jesus,

Relieve our anxiety around what we cannot control, discharge our doubt, and lighten our spiritual load so that we can trust You more! Amen.

The Back Up Plan

THE SYMPTOM

I feel so much confusion.

THE DIAGNOSIS

Systems fail because of a lack of solid plans.

THE PRESCRIPTION

Where there is no revelation, people cast off restraint;
but blessed is the one who heeds wisdom's instruction.
Proverbs 29:18

THE TREATMENT PLAN

I have had the privilege in the latter years of my ministry and leadership to do a lot of air travel. As a consequence, I had the fortunate opportunity to talk to one of the pilots that had just flown a flight with me on the last leg of my travel. I struck up a conversation as we both walked toward the baggage claim. As we were walking, I asked her, "How do you do it? You fly these planes in and out of airports, night after night, and day after day." She says to me, "That's easy. I am hands-on for the takeoffs and the landings of the flight, but once we reach a certain altitude, the autopilot kicks in."

"Autopilot," I said, "Oh really!" Then I asked how she deals with turbulence like we'd just endured on my flight. She told me that the autopilot has a backup system that detects problems in flight. The autopilot sends the data we need to the backup system to correct the issue in real time and keep us flying. "Over my years," she said, "I learned that the data don't lie. I've come to trust the backup system watching over me to rescue me in times of trouble."

This lesson can help us with our understanding of how God works within our lives. When one system begins to fail, there is a backup system that knows what we need. When government systems fail, when our financial systems fail, and even when our relationships fail, God becomes our back up system. And guess what, my friend! The data don't lie! Data is the Word of God, and it informs us and inspires us to know that we have a divine back up system. There is a divine backup system that kicks in when trouble seems to be at its worst, and it reminds us that God is still at work within our lives!

THE FOLLOW-UP

Dear El Elyon,

One who blesses without condition, grant us Your love to proceed without hesitation to receive Your grace, that we may be one with You! Amen.

Grey's Anatomy

THE SYMPTOM
No one sees how much I am struggling.

THE DIAGNOSIS
Many individuals don't have the proper tools to handle the challenges that come along with personal adversity.

THE PRESCRIPTION
Consider it pure joy, my brothers and sisters, whenever you face trials of many kinds, because you know that the testing of your faith produces perseverance. Let perseverance finish its work so that you may be mature and complete, not lacking anything.
James 1:2-4

THE TREATMENT PLAN
Shonda Rhimes is the creator, executive producer, and head writer of the medical drama series *Grey's Anatomy*. The television series focuses on a group of young doctors at Seattle Grace Mercy West Hospital, who began their careers at the facility as interns.

In season 16, episode 18, the focus is Andrew DeLuca, a distinguished doctor who has bipolar disorder. Those around him don't trust him because they don't know which Dr. DeLuca is going to show up on any given day. While he was working, he saw a little girl who fit the profile for human trafficking. He sounded the alarm, but another doctor dismissed DeLuca's concerns, fearing he was on the verge of an episode, and ordered him to go home and rest. DeLuca became belligerent, because he couldn't control what was going to happen with this teenage girl who he believed was being trafficked. Dr. Deluca was carried out by security only to discover later that he wasn't manic, but right about the little girl being trafficked.

To quote the main character, Meredith Grey, "The problem is, fairytales don't come true. It's the nightmares that always seem to become a reality."

Yes, in a real sense, you are not allowed to struggle with your humanity when the world around is policing your behavior based upon how it will protect its interests and benefit its illusion. As a consequence, you are left dealing with your dilemma, bargaining with your own behavior, and trading with your trauma because the system is not designed and equipped to deal with your mayhem.

You are drowning, but nobody can see your struggle. No one will see your efforts. No one will feel your pain and sorrow, but they all will see your mistakes. Please understand that you are not the totality of your mess-ups, but the beautiful tapestry of the struggle you must endure.

As a consequence, this might be your testimony! You are bent, but not broken. You are scarred, but not disfigured. You are sad, but not hopeless. You are tired, but not lifeless. You are afraid, but not powerless. You are angry, but not bitter. You are depressed, but not giving up! The struggle is part of the story!

I know you have been told that it has to be black or white, but the life that is lived is very much in the grey! When I think of *Grey's Anatomy* in a spiritual sense, it reminds me of our need to know why we are struggling spiritually and emotionally, so that eventually we can experience some deliverance in areas we thought were impossible. Yes, life is lived in the grey. Even though we aim to live free from error, every day you wake is a day that you will have to deal with the struggle. Understand that the experience of conflict is required to survive in life, because to stand up, you have to know what it means to fall. Embrace the *Grey's Anatomy* of your life and allow God to deliver you from what you can't do on your own!

THE FOLLOW-UP

Dear Eternal Father,

Bless You for keeping me, holding me, and including me in Your perfect will. Thank You for being an awesome wonder! Amen.

Special Coat

THE SYMPTOM

I don't feel covered and it causes me to feel insecure.

THE DIAGNOSIS

When you feel unprotected, it causes unnecessary alarm within your spirit!

THE PRESCRIPTION

I lift up my eyes to the mountains—
where does my help come from?
My help comes from the Lord,
the Maker of heaven and earth.
He will not let your foot slip—
he who watches over you will not slumber;
indeed, he who watches over Israel
will neither slumber nor sleep.
The Lord watches over you—
the Lord is your shade at your right hand.
the sun will not harm you by day,
nor the moon by night.
The Lord will keep you from all harm—
he will watch over your life;
the Lord will watch over your coming and going
both now and forevermore.
Psalm 121:1-8

THE TREATMENT PLAN

There was a little boy who was about 3 years old. He was always friendly, but this one particular day seemed to be rough for him. It was a dreary Saturday morning, and to make matters worse, it was pouring down rain. His mother wanted to run an errand to the grocery store, and she desired very much for her son to come along for the ride.

When she told him that she wanted him to go, he immediately began throwing a temper tantrum, because he was afraid of the rain. "The rain is going to get me!" he cried to his mom. He didn't want to leave the house, so he planted himself in the middle of the floor in full rebellion. The rain was pouring down hard, and his mother convinced him that if he would trust her, she would give something that would protect him from the rain. "It is a very special coat," she said in a conspiratorial tone. "It has superpowers."

Superpowers! He was intrigued; he started to wipe the tears off his face as she went to the closet and pulled out a bright blue coat. The coat was made of something special, she told him, and he finally agreed to wrap himself in the super coat and accompany his mother to the store. As they returned from their errand, the rain started to come down even harder, and he started to cry. "I'm going to get wet, Mommy," he said through the tears, "I know it."

Much to his surprise, when his mother helped him out of his special coat at home, there was not a drop of water on his clothing or skin. A puzzled look on his face, he said, "I don't understand. The water was hitting me hard, but I didn't get wet." She said, "Son, you are still dry because of the layer protection that was covering you. That unique coat was made to handle the storm. So when the rains come down hard against you, you can remain dry!" She said to him, "Baby, you can always stand in the storm when your life is adequately covered."

There is absolutely nothing that can take away the favor that lives on the inside of you when the power of God's Spirit has covered you! Yes, evil may be present itself, but it cannot penetrate you when you have been adequately covered. You may slip and fall sometimes, but get back up and remember that God's Spirit has covered you! There are some things that you can only learn in a storm. God's Spirit is made to handle the rain you are experiencing in your life until the storm runs out of the rain!

THE FOLLOW-UP

Dear Elohim,

Protect me when I am unsure, shield my faith, and guard my favor with the power that can only come from You! Amen.

Promise to Love

THE SYMPTOM

I hate myself.

THE DIAGNOSIS

It is hard to love when your heart is controlled by hate.

THE PRESCRIPTION

No, in all these things we are more than conquerors through him who loved us. For I am convinced that neither death nor life, neither angels nor demons, neither the present nor the future, nor any powers, neither height nor depth, nor anything else in all creation, will be able to separate us from the love of God that is in Christ Jesus our Lord.
Romans 8:37-39

THE TREATMENT PLAN

Many individuals spend an excessive amount of time trying to justify their existence and their humanity, and as a result they look for love in the wrong places and cause pain for themselves and others. Their behavior sometimes reflects arrogance when, in reality, they are insecure. They look overconfident to many, but internally they are broken beyond repair. Many of their relationships don't last long-term because they haven't let go of the baggage of unresolved issues from previous relationships. Quick fixes don't resolve long-developed habits, and it feels like a hopeless situation. However, the answer is closer than you think! Your happiness is not derived from people, prestige, or power; it comes from a place of knowing how to genuinely love yourself.

Yes, self-love is not found but decided. Just as with happiness, we often place the responsibility of loving ourselves on other people's shoulders. It is easy to play the "blame-game" and wonder why other people drain our energy, but the reality is that we are each responsible for keeping ourselves charged.

Loving yourself is a sacred responsibility that is yours alone. Regardless of what you say or what you do, you can opt for self-love in every given moment—even when you mess up. You can choose self-love because God decided to love you, unconditionally; and we are to love what He loves! You have to speak into your life words that affirm the kind of love only you can give yourself with the help of the Lord Jesus!

When you hate yourself for what you said, learn to love yourself anyway! When you should have kept your mouth shut, love yourself anyway. When you have ruined everything, love yourself anyway. You could've done better, but it didn't happen. Still love yourself. You messed up AGAIN. There is no excuse. Love yourself anyway. When you understand the power of loving yourself despite your hatred for yourself, it will give you the freedom to forgive what you have done. The blessing is that whatever you have done can't keep God from loving you even more! This blessing is Good News.

THE FOLLOW-UP

Dear Jehovah Shammah,

Teach me Your admiration, nurture my heart, feed my mind, and fill my spirit with Your unconditional love! Amen.

How Bad Do You Want It?

THE SYMPTOM

I become impulsive when it takes too long for me to reach my goals.

THE DIAGNOSIS

Many people abort their blessing when they try to receive it too quickly.

THE PRESCRIPTION

What, then, shall we say in response to these things? If God is for us, who can be against us?
Romans 8:31

THE TREATMENT PLAN

Everyone wants something out of life. I know a lot of people who want to get in shape, do great things, travel the world, live an adventure, leave a legacy behind, and do something extraordinary. But there's a big difference between saying you want something and wanting something bad enough that you do anything to obtain what you desire. So, allow me to ask this question: How bad do you want it? Chances are you worked hard, prayed over it, and did whatever you could to make it happen; whether it was a new business, new relationship, improved credit, or a new house. You found yourself wanting it more than anything.

But it's taking you longer than you anticipated. You've encountered some challenges along the way. And a part of you wants to give up, but another part of you is feeling desperate and impulsive. I need you to stop before this becomes a problem! If you want something so bad that it can cause you to step out of your character and sacrifice your integrity, it is not worth it. You are heading down a path of serious trouble. Nothing is worth sacrificing your dignity. Remember, what God has for you is for you! Work hard for it, yes! Sweat for it, yes! Dream about it, yes! Give up your self-respect and honor, absolutely not! A lack of uprightness will destroy your power, drive away your gifts, cause people who believe in you to leave, and keep others from forming relationships with you!

Nothing is worth giving up what makes your anointing and character matter. Please take a long look in the mirror and begin to rediscover why you started with the desire in the very first place. It is the process of recalling this pure motive that will cause you to reset your mind and your aspirations! Slow down and wait for it. It will come to pass, and God will never withhold it from you if it is within His will for your life!

THE FOLLOW-UP

Gracious God,

Work on my spirit, trade my ambition, and purchase my destiny with Your blood so that I will be patient to wait for the blessings to come. Amen.

Track and Field

THE SYMPTOM

I am having a hard time letting go of something that should be behind me.

THE DIAGNOSIS

Timing is everything, and not learning how to let go can be tragic.

THE PRESCRIPTION

And let us run with perseverance the race marked out for us, fixing our eyes on Jesus, the pioneer and perfecter of faith. For the joy set before him, he endured the cross, scorning its shame, and sat down at the right hand of the throne of God. Consider him who endured such opposition from sinners, so that you will not grow weary and lose heart.
Hebrews 12:1-3

THE TREATMENT PLAN

I have always been an athlete, from the days of my youth until now as an adult. The sport that I excelled at in high school was track and field. I love track and field. I loved being on the rubber track and having camaraderie with my classmates. I enjoyed participating in the long jump, 100-yard dash, and 200-yard dash. However, there was one race that I made sure I would train for; it was the four-by-four relay race. The 4×400-meter relay, or long relay, is an athletics track event in which teams consist of four runners who each complete 400 meters or one lap.

Unlike the 4×100-meter relay, runners in the 4×400 typically look back and grasp the baton from the incoming runner, due to the fatigue of the incoming runner, and the broader margins allowed by the longer distance of the race. Something happened to me when I would pass the baton in this race that made me pay careful attention. When I would run the middle leg of the race, I realized that the baton that I held in my hand was teaching me a valuable life lesson. I learned that while I was in the middle of a race, the baton I held could not get ahead by holding on to what was behind it. The baton began to speak to me back then, as I hope it is talking to you now. The lesson from the baton is that you can't reach what's in front of you until you let go of what's behind you.

It is crucial to release the past and all that comes along with it. It will hinder you from releasing your potential in your future. Moving on from the past also means stepping into the unknown future. It means having the determination to let go of what is familiar—positive or negative—and being vulnerable enough to embrace and learn from what's ahead. Now run your race!

THE FOLLOW-UP

Dear Jesus,

You are the author and finisher of my faith. Allow me to run with the endurance that my future will become brighter because I trust in You! Amen.

CPSIA information can be obtained
at www.ICGtesting.com
Printed in the USA
FSHW011525260820
73248FS